Bret Harte, Robert B Honeyman

Flip and Found at Blazing Star

Bret Harte, Robert B Honeyman

Flip and Found at Blazing Star

ISBN/EAN: 9783337023652

Printed in Europe, USA, Canada, Australia, Japan

Cover: Foto ©ninafisch / pixelio.de

More available books at **www.hansebooks.com**

FLIP

AND

FOUND AT BLAZING STAR

BY

BRET HARTE

BOSTON
HOUGHTON, MIFFLIN AND COMPANY
New York: 11 East Seventeenth Street
The Riverside Press, Cambridge
1882

CONTENTS.

FLIP: A CALIFORNIA ROMANCE.

FLIP: A CALIFORNIA ROMANCE.

CHAPTER I.

JUST where the red track of the Los Gatos road streams on and upward like the sinuous trail of a fiery rocket until it is extinguished in the blue shadows of the Coast Range, there is an embayed terrace near the summit, hedged by dwarf firs. At every bend of the heat-laden road the eye rested upon it wistfully; all along the flank of the mountain, which seemed to pant and quiver in the oven-like air, through rising dust, the slow creaking of dragging wheels, the monotonous cry of tired springs, and the muffled beat of plunging hoofs, it held out a promise of sheltered coolness and green silences beyond. Sunburned and anxious faces yearned toward it from the dizzy, swaying tops of stage-coaches, from lagging teams far below, from the blinding white canvas covers of "mountain schooners," and from scorching saddles that seemed to weigh down the scrambling, sweating animals beneath. But it would seem that the hope was vain, the promise illusive. When the terrace was reached it appeared not only to have caught and gathered all the heat of the valley below, but to have evolved a fire of its own from some hidden crater-like source unknown. Nevertheless, instead of prostrating and enervating man and beast, it was said to have induced the wildest exaltation. The heated air was filled and stifling with resinous exhalations. The delirious spices of balm, bay, spruce, juniper, yerba buena, wild syringa, and strange aromatic herbs as yet unclassified, distilled and evaporated in that mighty heat, and seemed to fire with a midsummer madness all who breathed their fumes. They stung, smarted, stimulated, intoxicated. It was said that the most jaded and foot-sore horses became furious and ungovernable under their influence; wearied teamsters and muleteers, who had exhausted their profanity in the ascent, drank fresh draughts of inspiration in this fiery air, extended their vocabulary, and created new and startling forms of objurgation. It is recorded that one bibulous stage-driver exhausted description and condensed its virtues in a single phrase: "Gin and ginger." This felicitous epithet, flung out in a generous comparison with his favorite drink, "rum and gum," clung to it ever after.

Such was the current comment on this vale of spices. Like most human criticism it was hasty and superficial. No one yet had been known to have penetrated deeply its mysterious recesses. It was still far below the summit and its wayside inn. It had escaped the intruding foot of hunter and prospector; and the inquisitive patrol of the county surveyor had only skirted its boundary. It remained for Mr. Lance Harriott to complete its exploration. His reasons for so doing were simple. He had made the journey thither underneath the stage-coach, and clinging to its axle. He had chosen this hazardous mode of conveyance at night, as the coach crept by his place of concealment in the wayside brush, to elude the sheriff of Monterey County and his posse, who were after him. He had not made himself known to his fellow-passengers as they already knew him as a gambler, an outlaw, and a desperado; he deemed it unwise to present himself in his newer reputation of a man who had just slain a brother gambler in a quarrel, and for whom a reward was offered. He slipped from the axle as the stage-coach swirled past the brushing branches of fir, and for an instant lay unnoticed, a scarcely distinguishable mound of dust in the broken furrows of the road. Then, more like a beast than a man, he crept on his hands and knees into the steaming underbrush. Here he lay still until the clatter of harness and the sound of voices faded in the distance. Had he been followed, it would have been difficult to detect in that inert mass of rags any semblance to a known form or figure. A hideous reddish mask of dust and clay obliterated his face; his hands were shapeless stumps exaggerated in his trailing sleeves. And when he rose, staggering like a drunken man, and plunged wildly into the recesses of the wood, a cloud of dust followed him, and pieces and patches of his frayed and rotten garments clung to the impeding branches. Twice he fell, but, maddened and upheld by the smarting spices and stimulating aroma of the air, he kept on his course.

Gradually the heat became less oppressive; once when he stopped and leaned exhaustedly against a sapling, he fancied he saw the zephyr he could not yet feel in the glittering and trembling of leaves in the distance before him. Again the deep stillness was moved with a faint sighing rustle, and he knew he must be nearing the edge of the thicket. The spell of silence thus broken was followed by a fainter, more musical interruption — the glassy tinkle of water! A step further his foot trembled on the verge of a slight ravine, still closely canopied by the interlacing boughs overhead. A tiny stream that he could have dammed with his hand yet lingered in this parched red gash in the hillside and trickled into a deep, irregular, well-like cavity, that again overflowed and sent its slight surplus on. It had been the luxurious retreat of many a spotted trout; it was to be the bath of Lance Harriott. Without a moment's hesitation, without removing a single garment, he slipped cautiously into it, as if fearful of losing a single drop. His head disappeared from the level of the bank; the solitude was again unbroken. Only two objects remained upon the edge of the ravine, — his revolver and tobacco pouch.

A few minutes elapsed. A fearless blue jay alighted on the bank and made a prospecting peck at the tobacco pouch. It yielded in favor of a gopher, who endeavored to draw it toward his hole, but in turn gave way to a red squirrel, whose attention was divided, however, between the pouch and the revolver, which he regarded with mischievous fascination. Then there was a splash, a grunt, a sudden dispersion of animated nature, and the head of Mr. Lance Harriott appeared above the bank. It was a startling transformation. Not only that he had, by this wholesale process, washed himself and his light "drill" garments entirely clean, but that he had, apparently by the same operation, morally cleansed *himself*, and left every stain and ugly blot of his late misdeeds and reputation in his bath. His face, albeit scratched here and there, was rosy, round, shining with irrepressible good humor and youthful levity. His large blue eyes were infantine in their innocent surprise and thoughtlessness. Dripping yet with water, and panting, he rested his elbows lazily on the bank, and became instantly absorbed with a boy's delight in the movements of the gopher, who, after the first alarm, returned cautiously to abduct the tobacco pouch. If any familiar had failed to detect Lance Harriott in this hideous masquerade of dust and grime and tatters, still less would any passing stranger have recognized in this blonde faun the possible outcast and murderer. And, when with a swirl of his spattering sleeve, he drove back the gopher in a shower of spray and leaped to the bank, he seemed to have accepted his felonious hiding-place as a mere picnicking bower.

A slight breeze was unmistakably permeating the wood from the west. Looking in that direction, Lance imagined that the shadow was less dark, and although the undergrowth was denser, he struck off carelessly toward it. As he went on, the wood became lighter and lighter; branches, and presently leaves, were painted against the vivid blue of the sky. He knew he must be near the summit, stopped, felt for his revolver, and then lightly put the few remaining branches aside.

The full glare of the noonday sun at first blinded him. When he could see more clearly, he found himself on the open western slope of the mountain, which in the Coast Range was seldom wooded. The spiced thicket stretched between him and the summit, and again between him and the stage road that plunges from the terrace, like forked lightning into the valley below. He could command all the approaches without being seen. Not that this seemed to occupy his thoughts or cause him any anxiety. His first act was to disencumber himself of his tattered coat; he then filled and lighted his pipe, and stretched himself full-length on the open hillside, as if to bleach in the fierce sun. While smoking he carelessly perused the fragment of a newspaper which had enveloped his tobacco, and being struck with some amusing paragraph, read it half aloud again to some imaginary auditor, emphasizing its humor with an hilarious slap upon his leg.

Possibly from the relaxation of fatigue and the bath, which had become a vapor one as he alternately rolled and dried himself in the baking grass, his eyes closed dreamily. He was awakened by the sound of voices. They were distant; they were vague; they approached no nearer. He rolled himself to the verge of the first precipitous grassy descent. There was another bank or plateau below him, and then a confused depth of olive shadows, pierced here and there by the spiked helmets of pines. There was no trace of habitation, yet the voices were those of some monotonous occupation, and Lance distinctly heard through them the click of crockery and the ring of some household utensil. It appeared to be the interjectional, half listless, half perfunctory, domestic dialogue of an old man and a girl, of which the words were unintelligible. Their voices indicated the solitude of the mountain, but without sadness; they were mysterious without being awe-inspiring. They might have uttered the dreariest commonplaces, but, in their vast isolation, they seemed musical and eloquent. Lance drew his first sigh, — they had suggested dinner.

Careless as his nature was, he was too cautious to risk detection in broad daylight. He contented himself for the present with endeavoring to locate that particular part of the depths from which the voices seemed to rise. It was more difficult, however, to select some other way of penetrating it than by the stage road. "They're bound to have a fire or show a light when it's dark," he reasoned, and, satisfied with that reflection, lay down again. Presently he began to amuse himself by tossing some silver coins in the air. Then his attention was directed to a spur of the Coast Range which had been sharply silhouetted against the cloudless western sky. Something intensely white, something so small that it was scarcely larger than the silver coin in his hand, was appearing in a slight cleft of the range.

While he looked it gradually filled and obliterated the cleft. In another moment the whole serrated line of mountain had disappeared. The dense, dazzling white, encompassing host began to pour over and down every ravine and pass of the coast. Lance recognized the sea-fog, and knew that scarcely twenty miles away lay the ocean — and safety! The drooping sun was now caught and hidden in its soft embraces. A sudden chill breathed over the mountain. He shivered, rose, and plunged again for very warmth into the spice-laden thicket. The heated balsamic air began to affect him like a powerful sedative; his hunger was forgotten in the languor of fatigue: he slumbered. When he awoke it was dark. He groped his way through the thicket. A few stars were shining directly above him, but beyond and below, everything was lost in the soft, white, fleecy veil of fog. Whatever light or fire might have betokened human habitation was hidden. To push on blindly would be madness; he could only wait for morning. It suited the outcast's lazy philosophy. He crept back again to his bed in the hollow and slept. In that profound silence and shadow, shut out from human association and sympathy by the ghostly fog, what torturing visions conjured up by remorse and fear should have pursued him? What spirit passed before him, or slowly shaped itself out of the infinite blackness of the wood? None. As he slipped gently into that blackness he remembered with a slight regret, some biscuits that were dropped from the coach by a careless luncheon-consuming passenger. That pang over, he slept as sweetly, as profoundly, as divinely, as a child.

CHAPTER II.

He awoke with the aroma of the woods still steeping his senses. His first instinct was that of all young animals; he seized a few of the young, tender green leaves of the yerba buena vine that crept over his mossy pillow and ate them, being rewarded by a half berry-like flavor that seemed to soothe the cravings of his appetite. The languor of sleep being still upon him, he lazily watched the quivering of a sunbeam that was caught in the canopying boughs above. Then he dozed again. Hovering between sleeping and waking, he became conscious of a slight movement among the dead leaves on the bank beside the hollow in which he lay. The movement appeared to be intelligent, and directed toward his revolver, which glittered on the bank. Amused at this evident return of his larcenious friend of the previous day, he lay perfectly still. The movement and rustle continued, but it now seemed long and undulating. Lance's eyes suddenly became set; he was intensely, keenly awake. It was not a snake, but the hand of a human arm, half hidden in the moss, groping for the weapon. In that flash of perception he saw that it was small, bare, and deeply freckled. In an instant he grasped it firmly, and rose to his feet, dragging to his own level as he did so, the struggling figure of a young girl.

"Leave me go!" she said, more ashamed than frightened.

Lance looked at her. She was scarcely more than fifteen, slight and lithe, with a boyish flatness of breast and back. Her flushed face and bare throat were absolutely peppered with minute brown freckles, like grains of spent gunpowder. Her eyes, which were large and gray, presented the singular spectacle of being also freckled, — at least they were shot through in pupil and cornea with tiny spots like powdered allspice. Her hair was even more remarkable in its tawny, deerskin color, full of lighter shades, and bleached to the faintest of blondes on the crown of her head, as if by the action of the sun. She had evidently outgrown her dress, which was made for a smaller child, and the too brief skirt disclosed a bare, freckled, and sandy desert of shapely limb, for which the darned stockings were equally too scant. Lance let his grasp slip from her thin wrist to her hand, and then with a good-humored gesture tossed it lightly back to her.

"I ain't a bit frightened," she said; "I'm not going to run away, — don't you fear."

"Glad to hear it," said Lance, with unmistakable satisfaction, " but why did you go for my revolver ? "

She flushed again and was silent. Presently she began to kick the earth at the roots of the tree, and said, as if confidentially to her foot, —

" I wanted to get hold of it before you did."

" You did ? — and why ? "

" Oh, you know why."

Every tooth in Lance's head showed that he did, perfectly. But he was discreetly silent.

" I did n't know what you were hiding there for," she went on, still addressing the tree, "and," looking at him sideways under her white lashes, " I did n't see your face."

This subtle compliment was the first suggestion of her artful sex. It actually sent the blood into the careless rascal's face, and for a moment confused him. He coughed. " So you thought you'd freeze on to that six-shooter of mine until you saw my hand?"

She nodded. Then she picked up a broken hazel branch, fitted it into the small of her back, threw her tanned bare arms over the ends of it, and expanded her chest and her biceps at the same moment. This simple action was supposed to convey an impression at once of ease and muscular force.

"Perhaps you'd like to take it now," said Lance, handing her the pistol.

"I've seen six-shooters before now," said the girl, evading the proffered weapon and its suggestion. "Dad has one, and my brother had two derringers before he was half as big as me."

She stopped to observe in her companion the effect of this capacity of her family to bear arms. Lance only regarded her amusedly. Presently she again spoke abruptly: —

"What made you eat that grass, just now?"

"Grass!" echoed Lance.

"Yes, there," pointing to the yerba buena.

Lance laughed. "I was hungry. Look!" he said, gayly tossing some silver into the air. "Do you think you could get me some breakfast for that, and have enough left to buy something for yourself?"

The girl eyed the money and the man with half-bashful curiosity.

"I reckon Dad might give ye suthing if he had a mind ter, though ez a rule he's down on tramps ever since they run off his chickens. Ye might try."

"But I want *you* to try. You can bring it to me here."

The girl retreated a step, dropped her eyes, and, with a smile that was a charming hesitation between bashfulness and impudence, said: "So you *are* hidin', are ye?"

"That's just it. Your head's level. I am," laughed Lance unconcernedly.

" Yur ain't one o' the McCarty gang — are ye ? "

Mr. Lance Harriott felt a momentary moral exaltation in declaring truthfully that he was not one of a notorious band of mountain freebooters known in the district under that name.

" Nor ye ain't one of them chicken lifters that raided Henderson's ranch ? We don't go much on that kind o' cattle yer."

" No," said Lance, cheerfully.

" Nor ye ain't that chap ez beat his wife unto death at Santa Clara ? "

Lance honestly scorned the imputation. Such conjugal ill treatment as he had indulged in had not been physical, and had been with other men's wives.

There was a moment's further hesitation on the part of the girl. Then she said shortly:

" Well, then, I reckon you kin come along with me."

"Where?" asked Lance.

"To the ranch," she replied simply.

"Then you won't bring me anything to eat here?"

"What for? You kin get it down there." Lance hesitated. "I tell you it's all right," she continued. "I'll make it all right with Dad."

"But suppose I reckon I'd rather stay here," persisted Lance, with a perfect consciousness, however, of affectation in his caution.

"Stay away then," said the girl coolly; "only as Dad perempted this yer woods"—

"*Pre*-empted," suggested Lance.

"Per-empted or pre-emp-ted, as you like," continued the girl scornfully,—"ez he's got a holt on this yer woods, ye might ez well see him down thar ez here. For here he's like to come any minit. You can bet your life on that."

She must have read Lance's amusement in his eyes, for she again dropped her own with a frown of brusque embarrassment. "Come along, then; I'm your man," said Lance, gayly, extending his hand.

She would not accept it, eying it, however, furtively, like a horse about to shy. "Hand me your pistol first," she said.

He handed it to her with an assumption of gayety. She received it on her part with unfeigned seriousness, and threw it over her shoulder like a gun. This combined action of the child and heroine, it is quite unnecessary to say, afforded Lance undiluted joy.

"You go first," she said.

Lance stepped promptly out, with a broad grin. "Looks kinder as if I was a prisner, don't it?" he suggested.

"Go on, and don't fool," she replied.

The two fared onward through the wood. For one moment he entertained the facetious idea of appearing to rush frantically away, "just to see what the girl would do," but abandoned it. "It's an even thing if she wouldn't spot me the first pop," he reflected admiringly.

When they had reached the open hillside, Lance stopped inquiringly. "This way," she said, pointing toward the summit, and in quite an opposite direction to the valley where he had heard the voices, one of which he now recognized as hers. They skirted the thicket for a few moments, and then turned sharply into a trail which began to dip toward a ravine leading to the valley.

"Why do you have to go all the way round?" he asked.

"*We* don't," the girl replied with emphasis; "there's a shorter cut."

"Where?"

"That's telling," she answered shortly.

"What's your name?" asked Lance, after a steep scramble and a drop into the ravine.

"Flip."

"What?"

"Flip."

"I mean your first name, — your front name."

"Flip."

"Flip! Oh, short for Felipa!"

"It ain't Flipper, — it's Flip." And she relapsed into silence.

"You don't ask me mine?" suggested Lance.

She did not vouchsafe a reply.

"Then you don't want to know?"

"Maybe Dad will. You can lie to *him*."

This direct answer apparently sustained the agreeable homicide for some moments. He moved onward, silently exuding admiration.

"Only," added Flip, with a sudden caution, "you'd better agree with me."

The trail here turned again abruptly and reëntered the cañon. Lance looked up, and noticed they were almost directly beneath the bay thicket and the plateau that towered far above them. The trail here showed signs of clearing, and the way was marked by felled trees and stumps of pines.

"What does your father do here?" he finally asked. Flip remained silent, swinging the revolver. Lance repeated his question.

"Burns charcoal and makes diamonds," said Flip, looking at him from the corners of her eyes.

"Makes diamonds?" echoed Lance.

Flip nodded her head.

"Many of 'em?" he continued carelessly.

"Lots. But they're not big," she returned, with a sidelong glance.

"Oh, they're not big?" said Lance gravely.

They had by this time reached a small staked inclosure, whence the sudden fluttering and cackle of poultry welcomed the return of the evident mistress of this sylvan retreat.

It was scarcely imposing. Further on, a cooking stove under a tree, a saddle and bridle, a few household implements scattered about, indicated the "ranch." Like most pioneer clearings, it was simply a disorganized raid upon nature that had left behind a desolate battle-field strewn with waste and decay. The fallen trees, the crushed thicket, the splintered limbs, the rudely torn-up soil, were made hideous by their grotesque juxtaposition with the wrecked fragments of civilization, in empty cans, broken bottles, battered hats, soleless boots, frayed stockings, cast-off rags, and the crowning absurdity of the twisted-wire skeleton of a hooped skirt hanging from a branch. The wildest defile, the densest thicket, the most virgin solitude, was less dreary and forlorn than this first footprint of man. The only redeeming feature of this prolonged bivouac was the cabin itself. Built of the half-cylindrical strips of pine bark, and thatched with the same material, it had a certain picturesque rusticity. But this was an accident of economy rather than taste, for which Flip apologized by saying that the bark of the pine was "no good" for charcoal.

"I reckon dad's in the woods," she added, pausing before the open door of the cabin. "Oh, Dad!" Her voice, clear and high, seemed to fill the whole long cañon, and echoed from the green plateau above. The monotonous strokes of an axe were suddenly pretermitted, and somewhere from the depths of the close-set pines a voice answered "Flip." There was a pause of a few moments, with some muttering, stumbling, and crackling in the underbrush, and then the sudden appearance of "Dad."

Had Lance first met him in the thicket, he would have been puzzled to assign his race to Mongolian, Indian, or Ethiopian origin. Perfunctory but incomplete washings of his hands and face, after charcoal burning, had gradually ground into his skin a grayish slate-pencil pallor, grotesquely relieved at the edges, where the washing had left off, with a border of a darker color. He looked like an overworked Christy minstrel with the briefest of intervals between his performances. There were black rims in the orbits of his eyes, as if he gazed feebly out of unglazed spectacles, which heightened his simian resemblance, already grotesquely exaggerated by what appeared to be repeated and spasmodic experiments in dyeing his gray hair. Without the slightest notice of Lance, he inflicted his protesting and querulous presence entirely on his daughter.

"Well! what's up now? Yer ye are calling me from work an hour before noon. Dog my skin, ef I ever get fairly limbered up afore it's 'Dad!' and 'Oh, Dad!'"

To Lance's intense satisfaction the girl received this harangue with an air of supreme indifference, and when " Dad " had relapsed into an unintelligible, and, as it seemed to Lance, a half-frightened muttering, she said coolly, —

" Ye 'd better drop that axe and scoot round getten' this stranger some breakfast and some grub to take with him. He 's one of them San Francisco sports out here trout fishing in the branch. He 's got adrift from his party, has lost his rod and fixins, and had to camp out last night in the Gin and Ginger Woods."

" That 's just it; it 's allers suthin like that," screamed the old man, dashing his fist on his leg in a feeble, impotent passion, but without looking at Lance. " Why in blazes don't he go up to that there blamed hotel on the summit? Why in thunder " — But here he caught his daughter's large, freckled eyes full in his own. He blinked feebly, his voice fell into a tone of whining entreaty. " Now, look yer, Flip, it's playing it rather low down on the old man, this yer running in o' tramps and desarted emigrants and cast-ashore sailors and forlorn widders and ravin' lunatics, on this yer ranch. I put it to you, Mister," he said abruptly, turning to Lance for the first time, but as if he had already taken an active part in the conversation, — "I put it as a gentleman yourself, and a fair-minded sportin' man, if this is the square thing?"

Before Lance could reply, Flip had already begun. "That's just it! D' ye reckon, being a sportin' man and an A 1 feller, he's goin' to waltz down inter that hotel, rigged out ez he is? D' ye reckon he's goin' to let his partners get the laugh onter him? D' ye reckon he's goin' to show his head outer this yer ranch till he can do it square? Not much! Go 'long. Dad, you're talking silly!"

The old man weakened. He feebly trailed his axe between his legs to a stump and sat down, wiping his forehead with his sleeve, and imparting to it the appearance of a slate with a difficult sum partly rubbed out. He looked despairingly at Lance. "In course," he said, with a deep sigh, "you naturally ain't got any money. In course you left your pocket-book, containing fifty dollars, under a stone, and can't find it. In course," he continued, as he observed Lance put his hand to his pocket, "you've only got a blank check on Wells, Fargo & Co. for a hundred dollars, and you'd like me to give you the difference?"

Amused as Lance evidently was at this, his absolute admiration for Flip absorbed everything else. With his eyes fixed upon the girl, he briefly assured the old man that he would pay for everything he wanted. He did this with a manner quite different from the careless, easy attitude he had assumed toward Flip; at least the quick-witted girl noticed it, and wondered if he was angry. It was quite true that ever since his eye had fallen upon another of his own sex, its glance had been less frank and careless. Certain traits of possible impatience, which might develop into man-slaying, were coming to the fore. Yet a word or a gesture of Flip's was sufficient to change that manner, and when, with the fretful assistance of her father, she had prepared a somewhat sketchy and primitive repast, he questioned the old man about diamond-making. The eye of Dad kindled.

"I want ter know how ye knew I was making diamonds," he asked, with a certain bashful pettishness not unlike his daughter's.

"Heard it in 'Frisco," replied Lance, with glib mendacity, glancing at the girl.

"I reckon they're gettin' sort of skeert down there — them jewelers," chuckled Dad, "yet it's in nater that their figgers will have to come down. It's only a question of the price of charcoal. I suppose they did n't tell you how I made the discovery?"

Lance would have stopped the old man's narrative by saying that he knew the story, but he wished to see how far Flip lent herself to her father's delusion.

"Ye see, one night about two years ago I had a pit o' charcoal burning out there, and tho' it had been a smouldering and a smoking and a blazing for nigh unto a month, somehow it did n't charcoal worth a cent. And yet, dog my skin, but the heat o' that er pit was suthin hidyus and frightful; ye could n't stand within a hundred yards of it, and they could feel it on the stage road three miles over yon, t'other side the mountain. There was nights when me and Flip had to take our blankets up the ravine and camp out all night, and the back of this yer hut shriveled up like that bacon. It was about as nigh on to hell as any sample ye kin get here. Now, mebbe you think I built that air fire? Mebbe you'll allow the heat was just the nat'ral burning of that pit?"

"Certainly," said Lance, trying to see Flip's eyes, which were resolutely averted.

"Thet's whar you'd be lyin'! That yar heat kem out of the bowels of the yearth,— kem up like out of a chimbley or a blast, and kep up that yar fire. And when she cools down a month after, and I got to strip her, there was a hole in the yearth, and a spring o' bilin', scaldin' water pourin' out of it ez big as your waist. And right in the middle of it was this yer." He rose with the instinct of a skillful *raconteur*, and whisked from under his bunk a chamois leather bag, which he emptied on the table before them. It contained a small fragment of native rock crystal, half-fused upon a petrified bit of pine. It was so glaringly truthful, so really what it purported to be, that the most unscientific woodman or pioneer would have understood it at a glance. Lance raised his mirthful eyes to Flip.

"It was cooled suddint,—stunted by the water," said the girl, eagerly. She stopped, and as abruptly turned away her eyes and her reddened face.

"That's it, that's just it," continued the old man. "Thar's Flip, thar, knows it; she ain't no fool!" Lance did not speak, but turned a hard, unsympathizing look upon the old man, and rose almost roughly. The old man clutched his coat. "That's it, ye see. The carbon's just turning to di'mens. And stunted. And why? 'Cos the heat was n't kep up long enough. Mebbe yer think I stopped thar? That ain't me. Thar's a pit out yar in the woods ez hez been burning six months; it hain't, in course, got the advantages o' the old one, for it's nat'ral heat. But I'm keeping that heat up. I've got a hole where I kin watch it every four hours. When the time comes, I'm thar! Don't you see? That's me! that's David Fairley, — that's the old man, — you bet!"

"That's so," said Lance, curtly. "And now, Mr. Fairley, if you'll hand me over a coat or a jacket till I can get past these fogs on the Monterey road, I won't keep you from your diamond pit." He threw down a handful of silver on the table.

"Ther's a deerskin jacket yer," said the old man, "that one o' them vaqueros left for the price of a bottle of whiskey."

"I reckon it would n't suit the stranger," said Flip, dubiously producing a much-worn, slashed, and braided vaquero's jacket. But it did suit Lance, who found it warm, and also had suddenly found a certain satisfaction in opposing Flip. When he had put it on, and nodded coldly to the old man, and carelessly to Flip, he walked to the door.

"If you're going to take the Monterey road, I can show you a short cut to it," said Flip, with a certain kind of shy civility.

The paternal Fairley groaned. "That's it; let the chickens and the ranch go to thunder, as long as there's a stranger to trapse round with; go on!"

Lance would have made some savage reply, but Flip interrupted. "You know yourself, Dad, it's a blind trail, and as that 'ere constable that kem out here hunting French Pete, could n't find it, and had to go round by the cañon, like ez not the stranger would lose his way, and have to come back!" This dangerous prospect silenced the old man, and Flip and Lance stepped into the road together. They walked on for some moments without speaking. Suddenly Lance turned upon his companion.

"You did n't swallow all that rot about the diamond, did you?" he asked, crossly.

Flip ran a little ahead, as if to avoid a reply.

"You don't mean to say that's the sort of hog wash the old man serves out to you regularly?" continued Lance, becoming more slangy in his ill temper.

"I don't know that it's any consarn o' yours what I think," replied Flip, hopping from boulder to boulder, as they crossed the bed of a dry watercourse.

"And I suppose you've piloted round and dry-nussed every tramp and dead beat you've met since you came here," continued Lance, with unmistakable ill humor. "How many have you helped over this road?"

"It's a year since there was a Chinaman chased by some Irishmen from the Crossing into the brush about yer, and he was too afeered to come out, and nigh most starved to death in thar. I had to drag him out and start him on the mountain, for you couldn't get him back to the road. He was the last one but *you*."

"Do you reckon it's the right thing for a girl like you to run about with trash of this kind, and mix herself up with all sorts of roughs and bad company?" said Lance.

Flip stopped short. "Look! if you're goin' to talk like Dad, I'll go back."

The ridiculousness of such a resemblance struck him more keenly than a consciousness of his own ingratitude. He hastened to assure Flip that he was joking. When he had made his peace they fell into talk again, Lance becoming unselfish enough to inquire into one or two facts concerning her life which did not immediately affect him. Her mother had died on the plains when she was a baby, and her brother had run away from home at twelve. She fully expected to see him again, and thought he might sometime stray into their cañon. "That is why, then, you take so much stock in tramps," said Lance. "You expect to recognize *him?*"

"Well," replied Flip, gravely, "there is suthing in *that*, and there's suthing in *this:* some o' these chaps might run across brother and do him a good turn for the sake of me."

"Like me, for instance?" suggested Lance.

"Like you. You'd do him a good turn, would n't you?"

"You bet!" said Lance, with a sudden emotion that quite startled him; "only don't you go to throwing yourself round promiscuously." He was half-conscious of an irritating sense of jealousy, as he asked if any of her *protégés* had ever returned.

"No," said Flip, "no one ever did. It shows," she added with sublime simplicity, "I had done 'em good, and they could get on alone. Don't it?"

"It does," responded Lance grimly. "Have you any other friends that come?"

"Only the Postmaster at the Crossing."

"The Postmaster?"

"Yes: he's reckonin' to marry me next year, if I'm big enough."

"And what do you reckon?" asked Lance earnestly.

Flip began a series of distortions with her shoulders, ran on ahead, picked up a few pebbles and threw them into the wood, glanced back at Lance with swimming mottled eyes, that seemed a piquant incarnation of everything suggestive and tantalizing, and said,

"That's telling."

They had by this time reached the spot where they were to separate. "Look," said Flip, pointing to a faint deflection of their path, which seemed, however, to lose itself in the underbrush a dozen yards away, "ther's your trail. It gets plainer and broader the further you get on, but you must use your eyes here, and get to know it well afore you get into the fog. Good-by."

"Good-by." Lance took her hand and drew her beside him. She was still redolent of the spices of the thicket, and to the young man's excited fancy seemed at that moment to personify the perfume and intoxication of her native woods. Half laughingly, half earnestly, he tried to kiss her: she struggled for some time strongly, but at the last moment yielded, with a slight return and the exchange of a subtle fire that thrilled him, and left him standing confused and astounded as she ran away. He watched her lithe, nymph-like figure disappear in the checkered shadows of the wood, and then he turned briskly down the half-hidden trail. His eyesight was keen, he made good progress, and was soon well on his way toward the distant ridge.

But Flip's return had not been as rapid. When she reached the wood she crept to its beetling verge, and looking across the cañon watched Lance's figure as it vanished and reappeared in the shadows and sinuosities of the ascent. When he reached the ridge the outlying fog crept across the summit, caught him in its embrace, and wrapped him from her gaze. Flip sighed, raised herself, put her alternate foot on a stump, and took a long pull at her too-brief stockings. When she had pulled down her skirt and endeavored once more to renew the intimacy that had existed in previous years between the edge of her petticoat and the top of her stockings, she sighed again, and went home.

CHAPTER III.

For six months the sea fogs monotonously came and went along the Monterey coast; for six months they beleaguered the Coast Range with afternoon sorties of white hosts that regularly swept over the mountain crest, and were as regularly beaten back again by the leveled lances of the morning sun. For six months that white veil which had once hidden Lance Harriott in its folds returned without him. For that amiable outlaw no longer needed disguise or hiding-place. The swift wave of pursuit that had dashed him on the summit had fallen back, and the next day was broken and scattered. Before the week had passed, a regular judicial inquiry relieved his crime of premeditation, and showed it to be a rude duel of two armed and equally desperate men. From a secure vantage in a seacoast town Lance challenged a trial by his peers, and, as an already prejudged man escaping from his executioners, obtained a change of venue. Regular justice, seated by the calm Pacific, found the action of an interior, irregular jury rash and hasty. Lance was liberated on bail.

The Postmaster at Fisher's Crossing had just received the weekly mail and express from San Francisco, and was engaged in examining it. It consisted of five letters and two parcels. Of these, three of the letters and the two parcels were directed to Flip. It was not the first time during the last six months that this extraordinary event had occurred, and the curiosity of the Crossing was duly excited. As Flip had never called personally for the letters or parcels, but had sent one of her wild, irregular scouts or henchmen to bring them, and as she was seldom seen at the Crossing or on the stage road, that curiosity was never satisfied. The disappointment to the Postmaster — a man past the middle age — partook of a sentimental nature. He looked at the letters and parcels; he looked at his watch; it was yet early, he could return by noon. He again examined the addresses; they were in the same handwriting as the previous letters. His mind was made up, he would deliver them himself. The poetic, soulful side of his mission was delicately indicated by a pale blue necktie, a clean shirt, and a small package of gingernuts, of which Flip was extravagantly fond.

The common road to Fairley's Ranch was by the stage turnpike to a point below the Gin and Ginger Woods, where the prudent horseman usually left his beast and followed the intersecting trail afoot. It was here that the Postmaster suddenly observed on the edge of the wood the figure of an elegantly-dressed woman; she was walking slowly, and apparently at her ease; one hand held her skirts lightly gathered between her gloved fingers, the other slowly swung a riding whip. Was it a picnic of some people from Monterey or Santa Cruz? The spectacle was novel enough to justify his coming nearer. Suddenly she withdrew into the wood; he lost sight of her; she was gone. He remembered, however, that Flip was still to be seen, and as the steep trail was beginning to tax all his energies, he was fain to hurry forward. The sun was nearly vertical when he turned into the cañon, and saw the bark roof of the cabin beyond. At almost the same moment Flip appeared, flushed and panting, in the road before him.

"You've got something for me," she said, pointing to the parcel and letter. Completely taken by surprise, the Postmaster mechanically yielded them up, and as instantly regretted it. "They're paid for," continued Flip, observing his hesitation.

"That's so," stammered the official of the Crossing, seeing his last chance of knowing the contents of the parcel vanish; "but I thought ez it's a valooable package, maybe ye might want to examine it to see that it was all right afore ye receipted for it."

"I'll risk it," said Flip, coolly, "and if it ain't right I'll let ye know."

As the girl seemed inclined to retire with her property, the Postmaster was driven to other conversation. "We ain't had the pleasure of seeing you down at the Crossing for a month o' Sundays," he began, with airy yet pronounced gallantry. "Some folks let on you was keepin' company with some feller like Bijah Brown, and you were getting a little too set up for the Crossing." The individual here mentioned being the county butcher, and supposed to exhibit his hopeless affection for Flip by making a long and useless divergence from his weekly route to enter the cañon for "orders," Flip did not deem it necessary to reply. "Then I allowed how ez you might have company," he continued; "I reckon there's some city folks up at the summit. I saw a mighty smart, fash'n'ble gal cavorting round. Hed no end o' style and fancy fixin's. That's my kind, I tell you. I just weaken on that sort o' gal," he continued, in the firm belief that he had awakened Flip's jealousy, as he glanced at her well-worn homespun frock, and found her eyes suddenly fixed on his own.

"Strange I ain't got to see her yet," she replied coolly, shouldering her parcel, and quite ignoring any sense of obligation to him for his extra-official act.

"But you might get to see her at the edge of the Gin and Ginger Woods," he persisted feebly, in a last effort to detain her; "if you 'll take a *pasear* there with me." Flip's only response was to walk on toward the cabin, whence, with a vague complimentary suggestion of "droppin' in to pass the time o' day" with her father, the Postmaster meekly followed.

The paternal Fairley, once convinced that his daughter's new companion required no pecuniary or material assistance from his hands, relaxed to the extent of entering into a querulous confidence with him, during which Flip took the opportunity of slipping away. As Fairley had that infelicitous tendency of most weak natures, to unconsciously exaggerate unimportant details in their talk, the Postmaster presently became convinced that the butcher was a constant and assiduous suitor of Flip's. The absurdity of his sending parcels and letters by post when he might bring them himself did not strike the official. On the contrary, he believed it to be a masterstroke of cunning. Fired by jealousy and Flip's indifference, he " deemed it his duty " — using that facile form of cowardly offensiveness — to betray Flip.

Of which she was happily oblivious. Once away from the cabin, she plunged into the woods, with the parcel swung behind her like a knapsack. Leaving the trail, she presently struck off in a straight line through cover and underbrush with the unerring instinct of an animal, climbing hand over hand the steepest ascent, or fluttering like a bird from branch to branch down the deepest declivity. She soon reached that part of the trail where the susceptible Postmaster had seen the fascinating unknown. Assuring herself she was not followed, she crept through the thicket until she reached a little waterfall and basin that had served the fugitive Lance for a bath. The spot bore signs of later and more frequent occupancy, and when Flip carefully removed some bark and brushwood from a cavity in the rock and drew forth various folded garments, it was evident she had used it as a sylvan dressing-room. Here she opened the parcel; it contained a small and delicate shawl of yellow China crêpe. Flip instantly threw it over her shoulders and stepped hurriedly toward the edge of the wood. Then she began to pass backward and forward before the trunk of a tree. At first nothing was visible on the tree, but a closer inspection showed a large pane of ordinary window glass stuck in the fork of the branches. It was placed at such a cunning angle against the darkness of the forest opening that it made a soft and mysterious mirror, not unlike a Claude Lorraine glass, wherein not only the passing figure of the young girl was seen, but the dazzling green and gold of the hillside, and the far-off silhouetted crests of the Coast Range.

But this was evidently only a prelude to a severer rehearsal. When she returned to the waterfall she unearthed from her stores a large piece of yellow soap and some yards of rough cotton "sheeting." These she deposited beside the basin and again crept to the edge of the wood to assure herself that she was alone. Satisfied that no intruding foot had invaded that virgin bower, she returned to her bath and began to undress. A slight wind followed her, and seemed to whisper to the circumjacent trees. It appeared to waken her sister naiads and nymphs, who, joining their leafy fingers, softly drew around her a gently moving band of trembling lights and shadows, of flecked sprays and inextricably mingled branches, and involved her in a chaste sylvan obscurity, veiled alike from pursuing god or stumbling shepherd. Within these hallowed precincts was the musical ripple of laughter and falling water, and at times the glimpse of a lithe brier-caught limb, or a ray of sunlight trembling over bright flanks, or the white austere outline of a childish bosom.

When she drew again the leafy curtain, and once more stepped out of the wood, she was completely transformed. It was the figure that had appeared to the Postmaster; the slight, erect, graceful form of a young woman modishly attired. It was Flip, but Flip made taller by the lengthened skirt and clinging habiliments of fashion. Flip freckled, but, through the cunning of a relief of yellow color in her gown, her piquant brown-shot face and eyes brightened and intensified until she seemed like a spicy odor made visible. I cannot affirm that the judgment of Flip's mysterious *modiste* was infallible, or that the taste of Mr. Lance Harriott, her patron, was fastidious; enough that it was picturesque, and perhaps not more glaring and extravagant than the color in which Spring herself had once clothed the sere hillside where Flip was now seated. The phantom mirror in the tree fork caught and held her with the sky, the green leaves, the sunlight and all the graciousness of her surroundings, and the wind gently tossed her hair and the gay ribbons of her gypsy hat. Suddenly she started. Some remote sound in the trail below, inaudible to any ear less fine than hers, arrested her breathing. She rose swiftly and darted into cover.

Ten minutes passed. The sun was declining; the white fog was beginning to creep over the Coast Range. From the edge of the wood Cinderella appeared, disenchanted, and in her homespun garments. The clock had struck — the spell was past. As she disappeared down the trail even the magic mirror, moved by the wind, slipped from the tree top to the ground, and became a piece of common glass.

CHAPTER IV.

The events of the day had produced a remarkable impression on the facial aspect of the charcoal-burning Fairley. Extraordinary processes of thought, indicated by repeated rubbing of his forehead, had produced a high light in the middle and a corresponding deepening of shadow at the sides, until it bore the appearance of a perfect sphere. It was this forehead that confronted Flip reproachfully as became a deceived comrade, menacingly as became an outraged parent in the presence of a third party and — a Postmaster!

"Fine doin's this, yer receivin' clandecent bundles and letters, eh?" he began. Flip sent one swift, withering look of contempt at the Postmaster, who at once becoming invertebrate and groveling, mumbled that he must "get on" to the Crossing, and rose to go. But the old man, who had counted on his presence for moral support, and was clearly beginning to hate him for precipitating this scene with his daughter, whom he feared, violently protested.

"Sit down, can't ye? Don't you see you're a witness?" he screamed hysterically.

It was a fatal suggestion. "Witness," repeated Flip, scornfully.

"Yes, a witness! He gave ye letters and bundles."

"Were n't they directed to me?" asked Flip.

"Yes," said the Postmaster, hesitatingly; "in course, yes."

"Do *you* lay claim to them?" she said, turning to her father.

"No," responded the old man.

"Do you?" sharply, to the Postmaster.

"No," he replied.

"Then," said Flip, coolly, "if you're not claimin' 'em for yourself, and you hear father say they ain't his, I reckon the less you have to say about 'em the better."

"Thar's suthin' in that," said the old man, shamelessly abandoning the Postmaster.

"Then why don't she say who sent 'em, and what they are like," said the Postmaster, "if there's nothin' in it?"

"Yes," echoed Dad. "Flip, why don't you?"

Without answering the direct question, Flip turned upon her father.

"Maybe you forget how you used to row and tear round here because tramps and such like came to the ranch for suthin', and I gave it to 'em? Maybe you'll quit tearin' round and letting yourself be made a fool of now by that man, just because one of those tramps gets up and sends us some presents back in turn?"

"'Twas n't me, Flip," said the old man, deprecatingly, but glaring at the astonished Postmaster. "'Twas n't my doin'. I allus said if you cast your bread on the waters it would come back to you by return mail. The fact is, the Gov'ment is gettin' too high-handed! Some o' these bloated officials had better climb down before next leckshen."

"Maybe," continued Flip to her father, without looking at her discomfited visitor, "ye 'd better find out whether one of those officials comes up to this yer 'ranch to steal away a gal about my own size, or to get points about diamond-making. I reckon he don't travel round to find out who writes all the letters that go through the Post Office."

The Postmaster had seemingly miscalculated the old man's infirm temper, and the daughter's skillful use of it. He was unprepared for Flip's boldness and audacity, and when he saw that both barrels of the accusation had taken effect on the charcoal burner, who was rising with epileptic rage, he fairly turned and fled. The old man would have followed him with objurgation beyond the door, but for the restraining hand of Flip.

Baffled and beaten, nevertheless Fate was not wholly unkind to the retreating suitor. Near the Gin and Ginger Woods he picked up a letter which had fallen from Flip's pocket. He recognized the writing, and did not scruple to read it. It was not a love epistle, — at least, not such a one as he would have written, — it did not give the address nor the name of the correspondent; but he read the following with greedy eyes: —

"Perhaps it's just as well that you don't rig yourself out for the benefit of those dead beats at the Crossing, or any tramp that might hang round the ranch. Keep all your style for me when I come. I can't tell you when, it's mighty uncertain before the rainy season. But I'm coming soon.

Don't go back on your promise about lettin' up on the tramps, and being a little more high-toned. And don't you give 'em so much. It's true I sent you hats *twice*. I clean forgot all about the first; but *I* would n't have given a ten-dollar hat to a nigger woman who had a sick baby because I had an extra hat. I'd have let that baby slide. I forgot to ask whether the skirt is worn separately; I must see that dressmaking sharp about it; but I think you'll want something on besides a jacket and skirt; at least, it looks like it up here. I don't think you could manage a piano down there without the old man knowing it, and raisin' the devil generally. I promised you I'd let up on him. Mind you keep all your promises to me. I'm glad you're gettin' on with the six-shooter; tin cans are good at fifteen yards, but try it on suthin' that *moves!* I forgot to say that I am on the track of your big brother. It's a three years' old track, and he was in Arizona. The friend who told me did n't expatiate much on what he did there, but I reckon they had a high old time. If he's above the earth I'll find him, you bet. The yerba buena and the southern wood came all right, — they smelt like you. Say, Flip, do you remember the *last* — the *very last* — thing that happened when you said 'Good-by' on the trail? Don't let me ever find out that you 've let anybody else kiss " —

But here the virtuous indignation of the Postmaster found vent in an oath. He threw the letter away. He retained of it only two facts, — Flip *had* a brother who was missing; she had a lover present in the flesh.

How much of the substance of this and previous letters Flip had confided to her father I cannot say. If she suppressed anything it was probably that which affected Lance's secret alone, and it was doubtful how much of that she herself knew. In her own affairs she was frank without being communicative, and never lost her shy obstinacy even with her father. Governing the old man as completely as she did, she appeared most embarrassed when she was most dominant; she had her own way without lifting her voice or her eyes; she seemed oppressed by *mauvaise honte* when she was most triumphant; she would end a discussion with a shy murmur addressed to herself, or a single gesture of self-consciousness.

The disclosure of her strange relations with an unknown man, and the exchange of presents and confidences seemed to suddenly awake Fairley to a vague, uneasy sense of some unfulfilled duties as a parent. The first effect of this on his weak nature, was a peevish antagonism to the cause of it. He had long, fretful monologues on the vanity of diamond-making, if accompanied with " pestering " by " interlopers; " on the wickedness of concealment and conspiracy, and their effects on charcoal-burning; on the nurturing of spies and " adders " in the family circle, and on the seditiousness of dark and mysterious councils in which a gray-haired father was left out. It was true that a word or look from Flip generally brought these monologues to an inglorious and abrupt termination, but they were none the less lugubrious as long as they lasted. In time they were succeeded by an affectation of contrite apology and self-depreciation. "Don't go out o' the way to ask the old man," he would say, referring to the quantity of bacon to be ordered; "it's nat'ral a young gal should have her own advisers." The state of the flour barrel would also produce a like self-abasement. "Unless ye're already in correspondence about more flour, ye might take the opinion o' the first tramp ye meet ez to whether Santa Cruz Mills is a good brand, but don't ask the old man." If Flip was in conversation with the butcher, Fairley would obtrusively retire with the hope "he wasn't intrudin' on their secrets."

These phases of her father's weakness were not frequent enough to excite her alarm, but she could not help noticing they were accompanied with a seriousness unusual to him. He began to be tremulously watchful of her, returning often from work at an earlier hour, and lingering by the cabin in the morning. He brought absurd and useless presents for her, and presented them with a nervous anxiety, poorly concealed by an assumption of careless, paternal generosity. "Suthin' I picked up at the Crossin' for ye to-day," he would say, airily, and retire to watch the effect of a pair of shoes two sizes too large, or a fur cap in September. He would have hired a cheap parlor organ for her, but for the apparently unexpected revelation that she could n't play. He had received the news of a clue to his long-lost son without emotion, but lately he seemed to look upon it as a foregone conclusion, and one that necessarily solved the question of companionship for Flip. "In course, when you've got your own flesh and blood with ye, ye can't go foolin' around with strangers." These autumnal blossoms of affection, I fear, came too late for any effect upon Flip, precociously matured by her father's indifference and selfishness. But she was good humored, and, seeing him seriously concerned, gave him more of her time, even visited him in the sacred seclusion of the " diamond pit," and listened with far-off eyes to his fitful indictment of all things outside his grimy laboratory. Much of this patient indifference came with a capricious change in her own habits; she no longer indulged in the rehearsal of dress, she packed away her most treasured garments, and her leafy boudoir knew her no more. She sometimes walked on the hillside, and often followed the trail she had taken with Lance when she led him to the ranch. She once or twice extended her walk to the spot where she had parted from him, and as often came shyly away, her eyes downcast and her face warm with color. Perhaps because these experiences and some mysterious instinct of maturing womanhood had left a story in her eyes, which her two adorers, the Postmaster and the Butcher, read with passion, she became famous without knowing it. Extravagant stories of her fascinations brought strangers into the valley. The effect upon her father may be imagined. Lance could not have desired a more effective guardian than he proved to be in this emergency. Those who had been told of this hidden pearl were surprised to find it so jealously protected.

CHAPTER V.

THE long, parched summer had drawn to its dusty close. Much of it was already blown abroad and dissipated on trail and turnpike, or crackled in harsh, unelastic fibres on hillside and meadow. Some of it had disappeared in the palpable smoke by day and fiery crests by night of burning forests. The besieging fogs on the Coast Range daily thinned their hosts, and at last vanished. The wind changed from northwest to southwest. The salt breath of the sea was on the summit. And then one day the staring, unchanged sky was faintly touched with remote mysterious clouds, and grew tremulous in expression. The next morning dawned upon a newer face in the heavens, on changed woods, on altered outlines, on vanished crests, on forgotten distances. It was raining!

Four weeks of this change, with broken spaces of sunlight and intense blue aerial islands, and then a storm set in. All day the summit pines and redwoods rocked in the blast. At times the onset of the rain seemed to be held back by the fury of the gale, or was visibly seen in sharp waves on the hillside. Unknown and concealed watercourses suddenly overflowed the trails, pools became lakes and brooks rivers. Hidden from the storm, the sylvan silence of sheltered valleys was broken by the impetuous rush of waters; even the tiny streamlet that traversed Flip's retreat in the Gin and Ginger Woods became a cascade.

The storm drove Fairley from his couch early. The falling of a large tree across the trail, and the sudden overflow of a small stream beside it, hastened his steps. But he was doomed to encounter what was to him a more disagreeable object — a human figure. By the bedraggled drapery that flapped and fluttered in the wind, by the long, unkempt hair that hid the face and eyes, and by the grotesquely misplaced bonnet, the old man recognized one of his old trespassers, — an Indian squaw.

"Clear out 'er that! Come, make tracks, will ye?" the old man screamed; but here the wind stopped his voice, and drove him against a hazel bush.

"Me heap sick," answered the squaw, shivering through her muddy shawl.

"I'll make ye a heap sicker if ye don't vamose the ranch," continued Fairley, advancing.

"Me wantee Wangee girl. Wangee girl give me heap grub," said the squaw, without moving.

"You bet your life," groaned the old man

to himself. Nevertheless an idea struck him. "Ye ain't brought no presents, hev ye?" he asked cautiously. "Ye ain't got no pooty things for poor Wangee girl?" he continued, insinuatingly.

"Me got heap *cache* nuts and berries," said the squaw.

"Oh, in course! in course! That's just it," screamed Fairley; "you've got 'em *cached* only two mile from yer, and you'll go and get 'em for a half dollar, cash down."

"Me bring Wangee girl to *cache*," replied the Indian, pointing to the wood. "Honest Injin."

Another bright idea struck Mr. Fairley. But it required some elaboration. Hurrying the squaw with him through the pelting rain, he reached the shelter of the corral. Vainly the shivering aborigine drew her tightly bandaged papoose closer to her square, flat breast, and looked longingly toward the cabin; the old man backed her against the palisade. Here he cautiously imparted his dark intentions to employ her to keep watch and ward over the ranch, and especially over its young mistress — " clear out all the tramps 'ceptin' yourself, and I'll keep ye in grub and rum." Many and deliberate repetitions of this offer in various forms at last seemed to affect the squaw; she nodded violently, and echoed the last word " rum." " Now," she added. The old man hesitated; she was in possession of his secret; he groaned, and, promising an immediate installment of liquor, led her to the cabin.

The door was so securely fastened against the impact of the storm that some moments elapsed before the bar was drawn, and the old man had become impatient and profane. When it was partly opened by Flip he hastily slipped in, dragging the squaw after him, and cast one single suspicious glance around the rude apartment which served as a sitting-room. Flip had apparently been writing. A small inkstand was still on the board table, but her paper had evidently been concealed before she allowed them to enter. The squaw instantly squatted before the adobe hearth, warmed her bundled baby, and left the ceremony of introduction to her companion. Flip regarded the two with calm preoccupation and indifference. The only thing that touched her interest was the old squaw's draggled skirt and limp neckerchief. They were Flip's own, long since abandoned and cast off in the Gin and Ginger Woods. "Secrets again," whined Fairley, still eying Flip furtively. "Secrets again, in course — in course — jiss so. Secrets that must be kep from the ole man. Dark doin's by one's own flesh and blood. Go on! go on! Don't mind me." Flip did not reply. She had even lost the interest in her old dress. Perhaps it had only touched some note in unison with her revery.

"Can't ye get the poor critter some whiskey?" he queried, fretfully. "Ye used to be peart enuff before." As Flip turned to the corner to lift the demijohn, Fairley took occasion to kick the squaw with his foot, and indicate by extravagant pantomime that the bargain was not to be alluded to before the girl. Flip poured out some whiskey in a tin cup, and, approaching the squaw, handed it to her. "It's like ez not," continued Fairley to his daughter, but looking at the squaw, "that she'll be huntin' the woods off and on, and kinder looking after the last pit near the *Madroños;* ye'll give her grub and licker ez she likes. Well, d' ye hear, Flip? Are ye moonin' agin with yer secrets? What's gone with ye?"

If the child were dreaming, it was a delicious dream. Her magnetic eyes were suffused by a strange light, as though the eye itself had blushed; her full pulse showed itself more in the rounding outline of her cheek than in any deepening of color; indeed, if there was any heightening of tint, it was in her freckles, which fairly glistened like tiny spangles. Her eyes were downcast, her shoulders slightly bent, but her voice was low and clear and thoughtful as ever.

"One o' the big pines above the *Madroño* pit has blown over into the run," she said. "It's choked up the water, and it's risin' fast. Like ez not it's pourin' over into the pit by this time."

The old man rose with a fretful cry. "And why in blazes didn't you say so first?" he screamed, catching up his axe and rushing to the door.

"Ye didn't give me a chance," said Flip, raising her eyes for the first time. With an impatient imprecation, Fairley darted by her and rushed into the wood. In an instant she had shut the door and bolted it. In the same instant the squaw arose, dashed the long hair not only from her eyes, but from her head, tore away her shawl and blanket, and revealed the square shoulders of Lance Harriott! Flip remained leaning against the door; but the young man in rising dropped the bandaged papoose, which rolled from his lap into the fire. Flip, with a cry, sprang toward it; but Lance caught her by the waist with one arm, as with the other he dragged the bundle from the flames.

"Don't be alarmed," he said, gayly, "it's only"—

"What?" said Flip, trying to disengage herself.

"My coat and trousers."

Flip laughed, which encouraged Lance to another attempt to kiss her. She evaded it by diving her head into his waistcoat, and saying, "There's father."

"But he's gone to clear away that tree?" suggested Lance.

One of Flip's significant silences followed.

"Oh, I see," he laughed. "That was a plan to get him away! Ah!" She had released herself.

"Why did you come like that?" she said, pointing to his wig and blanket.

"To see if you'd know me," he responded.

"No," said Flip, dropping her eyes. "It's to keep other people from knowing you. You're hidin' agin."

"I am," returned Lance; "but," he interrupted, "it's only the same old thing."

"But you wrote from Monterey that it was all over," she persisted.

"So it would have been," he said gloomily, "but for some dog down here who is hunting up an old scent. I'll spot him yet, and"— He stopped suddenly, with such utter abstraction of hatred in his fixed and glittering eyes that she almost feared him. She laid her hand quite unconsciously on his arm. He grasped it; his face changed.

"I couldn't wait any longer to see you, Flip, so I came here anyway," he went on. "I thought to hang round and get a chance to speak to you first, when I fell afoul of the old man. He didn't know me, and tumbled right in my little game. Why, do you believe he wants to hire me for my grub and liquor, to act as a sort of sentry over you and the ranch?" And here he related with great gusto the substance of his interview. "I reckon as he's that suspicious," he concluded, "I'd better play it out now as I've begun, only it's mighty hard I can't see you here before the fire in your fancy toggery, Flip, but must dodge in and out of the wet underbrush in these yer duds of yours that I picked up in the old place in the Gin and Ginger Woods."

"Then you came here just to see me?" asked Flip.

"I did."

"For only that?"

"Only that."

Flip dropped her eyes. Lance had got his other arm around her waist, but her resisting little hand was still potent.

"Listen," she said at last without looking up, but apparently talking to the intruding arm, "when Dad comes I'll get him to send you to watch the diamond pit. It isn't far; it's warm, and"—

"What?"

"I'll come, after a bit, and see you. Quit foolin' now. If you'd only have come here like yourself — like — like — a white man."

"The old man," interrupted Lance, "would have just passed me on to the summit. I couldn't have played the lost fisherman on him at this time of year."

"Ye could have been stopped at the Crossing by high water, you silly," said the girl.

"It was." This grammatical obscurity referred to the stage coach.

"Yes, but I might have been tracked to this cabin. And look here, Flip," he said, suddenly straightening himself, and lifting the girl's face to a level with his own, "I don't want you to lie any more for me. It ain't right."

"All right. Ye need n't go to the pit, then, and I won't come."

"Flip!"

"And here's Dad coming. Quick!"

Lance chose to put his own interpretation on this last adjuration. The resisting little hand was now lying quite limp on his shoulder. He drew her brown, bright face near his own, felt her spiced breath on his lips, his cheeks, his hot eyelids, his swimming eyes, kissed her, hurriedly replaced his wig and blanket, and dropped beside the fire with the tremulous laugh of youth and innocent first passion. Flip had withdrawn to the window, and was looking out upon the rocking pines.

"He don't seem to be coming," said Lance, with a half-shy laugh.

"No," responded Flip demurely, pressing her hot oval cheek against the wet panes; "I reckon I was mistaken. You're sure," she added, looking resolutely another way, but still trembling like a magnetic needle toward Lance, as he moved slightly before the fire, "you're *sure* you'd like me to come to you?"

"Sure, Flip?"

"Hush!" said Flip, as this reassuring query of reproachful astonishment appeared about to be emphasized by a forward amatory dash of Lance's; "hush! he's coming this time, sure."

It was, indeed, Fairley, exceedingly wet, exceedingly bedraggled, exceedingly sponged out as to color, and exceedingly profane. It appeared that there was, indeed, a tree that had fallen in the "run," but that, far from diverting the overflow into the pit, it had established "back water," which had forced another outlet. All this might have been detected at once by any human intellect not distracted by correspondence with strangers, and enfeebled by habitually scorning the intellect of its own progenitor. This reckless selfishness had further only resulted in giving "rheumatics" to that progenitor, who now required the external administration of opodeldoc to his limbs, and the internal administration of whiskey. Having thus spoken, Mr. Fairley, with great promptitude and infantine simplicity, at once bared two legs of entirely different colors and mutely waited for his daughter to rub them. If Flip did this all unconsciously, and with the mechanical dexterity of previous habit, it was because she did not quite understand the savage eyes and impatient gestures of Lance in his encompassing wig and blanket, and because it helped her to voice her thought.

"Ye'll never be able to take yer watch at the diamond pit to-night, Dad," she said; "and I've been reck'nin' you might set the squaw there instead. I can show her what to do."

But to Flip's momentary discomfiture, her father promptly objected. "Mebbee I've got suthin' else for her to do. Mebbee I may have my secrets, too — eh?" he said, with dark significance, at the same time administering a significant nudge to Lance, which kept up the young man's exasperation. "No, she'll rest yer a bit just now. I'll set her to watchin' suthin' else, like as not, when I want her." Flip fell into one of her suggestive silences. Lance watched her earnestly, mollified by a single furtive glance from her significant eyes; the rain dashed against the windows, and occasionally spattered and hissed in the hearth of the broad chimney, and Mr. David Fairley, somewhat assuaged by the internal administration of whiskey, grew more loquacious. The genius of incongruity and inconsistency which generally ruled his conduct came out with freshened vigor under the gentle stimulation of spirit. "On an evening like this," he began, comfortably settling himself on the floor beside the chimney, " ye might rig yerself out in them new duds and fancy fixin's that that Sacramento shrimp sent ye, and let your own flesh and blood see ye. If that's too much to do for your old dad, ye might do it to please that digger squaw as a Christian act." Whether in the hidden depths of the old man's consciousness there was a feeling of paternal vanity in showing this wretched aborigine the value and importance of the treasure she was about to guard, I cannot say. Flip darted an interrogatory look at Lance, who nodded a quiet assent, and she flew into the inner room. She did not linger on the details of her toilet, but reappeared almost the next moment in her new finery, buttoning the neck of her gown as she entered the room, and chastely stopping at the window to characteristically pull up her stocking. The peculiarity of her situation increased her usual shyness; she played with the black and gold beads of a handsome necklace, — Lance's last gift, — as the merest child might; her unbuckled shoe gave the squaw a natural opportunity of showing her admiration and devotion by insisting upon buckling it, and gave Lance, under that disguise, an opportunity of covertly kissing the little foot and ankle in the shadow of the chimney; an event which provoked slight hysterical symptoms in Flip, and caused her to sit suddenly down in spite of the remonstrances of her parent. "Ef you can't quit gigglin' and squirmin' like an Injin baby yourself, ye'd better git rid o' them duds," he ejaculated with peevish scorn.

Yet, under this perfunctory rebuke, his weak vanity could not be hidden, and he enjoyed the evident admiration of a creature whom he believed to be half-witted and degraded all the more keenly because it did not make him jealous. She could not take Flip from him. Rendered garrulous by liquor, he went to voice his contempt for those who might attempt it. Taking advantage of his daughter's absence to resume her homely garments, he whispered confidentially to Lance, —

"Ye see these yer fine dresses, ye might think is presents. Pr'aps Flip lets on they are? Pr'aps she don't know any better. But they ain't presents. They're only samples o' dressmaking and jewelry that a vain, conceited shrimp of a feller up in Sacramento sends down here to get customers for. In course I'm to pay for 'em. In course he reckons I'm to do it. In course I calkilate to do it; but he need n't try to play 'em off as presents. He talks suthin' o' coming down here, sportin' hisself off on Flip as a fancy buck! Not ez long ez the old man's here, you bet." Thoroughly carried away by his fancied wrongs, it was perhaps fortunate that he did not observe the flashing eyes of Lance behind his lank and lustreless wig; but seeing only the figure of Lance, as he had conjured him, he went on: " That's why I want you to hang around her. Hang around her ontil my boy, — him that's comin' home on a visit, — gets here, and I reckon he'll clear out that yar Sacramento counter-jumper. Only let me get a sight o' him afore Flip does. Eh? D'ye hear? Dog my skin if I don't believe the d—d Injin's drunk." It was fortunate that at that moment Flip reappeared, and, dropping on the hearth between her father and the infuriated Lance, let her hand slip in his with a warning pressure. The light touch momentarily recalled him to himself and her, but not until the quick-witted girl had had revealed to her in one startled wave of consciousness, the full extent of Lance's infirmity of temper. With the instinct of awakened tenderness came a sense of responsibility, and a vague premonition of danger. The coy blossom of her heart was scarce unfolded before it was chilled by approaching shadows. Fearful of, she knew not what, she hesitated. Every moment of Lance's stay was imperiled by a single word that might spring from his suppressed white lips; beyond and above the suspicions his sudden withdrawal might awaken in her father's breast, she was dimly conscious of some mysterious terror without that awaited him. She listened to the furious onslaught of the wind upon the sycamores beside their cabin, and thought she heard it there; she listened to the sharp fusillade of rain upon roof and pane, and the turbulent roar and rush of leaping mountain torrents at their very feet, and fancied it was there. She suddenly sprang to the window, and, pressing her eyes to the pane, saw through the misty turmoil of tossing boughs and swaying branches the scintillating intermittent flames of torches moving on the trail above, and *knew* it was there!

In an instant she was collected and calm. "Dad," she said, in her ordinary indifferent tone, "there's torches movin' up toward the diamond pit. Likely it's tramps. I'll take the squaw and see." And before the old man could stagger to his feet she had dragged Lance with her into the road.

CHAPTER VI.

The wind charged down upon them, slamming the door at their backs, extinguishing the broad shaft of light that had momentarily shot out into the darkness, and swept them a dozen yards away. Gaining the lee of a madroño tree, Lance opened his blanketed arms, enfolded the girl, and felt her for one brief moment tremble and nestle in his bosom like some frightened animal. "Well," he said, gayly, "what next?" Flip recovered herself. "You're safe now anywhere outside the house. But did you expect them to-night?" Lance shrugged his shoulders. "Why not?" "Hush!" returned the girl; "they're coming this way."

The four flickering, scattered lights presently

dropped into line. The trail had been found; they were coming nearer. Flip breathed quickly; the spiced aroma of her presence filled the blanket as he drew her tightly beside him. He had forgotten the storm that raged around them, the mysterious foe that was approaching, until Flip caught his sleeve with a slight laugh. "Why, it's Kennedy and Bijah?"

"Who's Kennedy and Bijah?" asked Lance, curtly.

"Kennedy's the Postmaster and Bijah's the Butcher."

"What do they want?" continued Lance.

"Me," said Flip, coyly.

"You?"

"Yes; let's run away."

Half leading, half dragging her friend, Flip made her way with unerring woodcraft down the ravine. The sound of voices and even the tumult of the storm became fainter, an acrid smell of burning green wood smarted Lance's lips and eyes; in the midst of the darkness beneath him gradually a faint, gigantic nimbus like a lurid eye glowed and sank, quivered and faded with the spent breath of the gale as it penetrated their retreat. "The pit," whispered Flip; "it's safe on the other side," she added, cautiously skirting the orbit of the great eye, and leading him to a sheltered nest of bark and sawdust. It was warm and odorous. Nevertheless, they both deemed it necessary to enwrap themselves in the single blanket. The eye beamed fitfully upon them, occasionally a wave of lambent tremulousness passed across it; its weirdness was an excuse for their drawing nearer each other in playful terror.

"Flip."

"Well?"

"What did the other two want? To see you, *too?*"

"Likely," said Flip, without the least trace of coquetry. "There's been a lot of strangers yer, off and on."

"Perhaps you'd like to go back and see them?"

"Do you want me to?"

Lance's reply was a kiss. Nevertheless he was vaguely uneasy. "Looks a little as if I were running away, don't it?" he suggested.

"No," said Flip; "they think you're only a squaw; it's me they're after." Lance smarted a little at this infelicitous speech. A strange and irritating sensation had been creeping over him — it was his first experience of shame and remorse. "I reckon I'll go back and see," he said, rising abruptly.

Flip was silent. She was thinking. Believing that the men were seeking her only, she knew that their attention would be directed from her companion when it was found out he was no longer with her, and she dreaded to meet them in his irritable presence.

"Go," she said, "tell Dad something's gone wrong in the diamond pit, and say I'm watching it for him here."

"And you?"

"I'll go there and wait for him. If he can't get rid of them, and they follow him there, I'll come back here and meet you. Anyhow, I'll manage to have Dad wait there a spell."

She took his hand and led him back by a different path to the trail. He was surprised to find that the cabin, its window glowing from the fire, was only a hundred yards away. "Go in the back way, by the shed. Don't go in the room, nor near the light, if you can. Don't talk inside, but call or beckon to Dad. Remember," she said, with a laugh, "you're keeping watch of me for him. Pull your hair down on your eyes so." This operation, like most feminine embellishments of the masculine toilet was attended by a kiss, and Flip, stepping back into the shadow, vanished in the storm.

Lance's first movements were inconsistent with his assumed sex. He picked up his draggled skirt, and drew a bowie knife from his boot. From his bosom he took a revolver, turning the chambers noiselessly as he felt the caps. He then crept toward the cabin softly and gained the shed. It was quite dark but for a pencil of light piercing a crack of the rude, ill-fitting door that opened on the sitting room. A single voice not unfamiliar to him, raised in half-brutal triumph, greeted his ears. A name was mentioned — his own! His angry hand was on the latch. One moment more and he would have burst the door, but in that instant another name was uttered — a name that dropped his hand from the latch and the blood from his cheeks. He staggered backward, passed his hand swiftly across his forehead, recovered himself with a gesture of mingled rage and despair, and, sinking on his knees beside the door, pressed his hot temples against the crack.

"Do I know Lance Harriott?" said the voice. "Do I know the d——d ruffian? Didn't I hunt him a year ago into the brush three miles from the Crossing? Didn't we lose sight of him the very day he turned up yer at this ranch, and got smuggled over into Monterey? Ain't it the same man as killed Arkansaw Bob — Bob Ridley — the name he went by in Sonora? And who was Bob Ridley, eh? Who? Why, you d——d old fool, it was Bob Fairley — YOUR SON!"

The old man's voice rose querulous and indistinct.

"What are ye talkin' about?" interrupted the first speaker. "I tell you I *know*. Look at these pictures. I found 'em on his body.

Look at 'em. Pictures of you and your girl. Pr'aps you'll deny them. Pr'aps you'll tell me I lie when I tell you *he* told me he was your son; told me how he ran away from you; how you were livin' somewhere in the mountains makin' gold, or suthin' else, outer charcoal. He told me who he was as a secret. He never let on he told it to any one else. And when I found that the man who killed him, Lance Harriott, had been hidin' here, had been sendin' spies all around to find out all about your son, had been foolin' you and tryin' to ruin your gal as he had killed your boy, I knew that *he* knew it too."

"LIAR!"

The door fell in with a crash. There was the sudden apparition of a demoniac face, still half hidden by the long trailing black locks of hair that curled like Medusa's around it. A cry of terror filled the room. Three of the men dashed from the door and fled precipitately. The man who had spoken sprang toward his rifle in the chimney corner. But the movement was his last; a blinding flash and shattering report interposed between him and his weapon. The impulse carried him forward headlong into the fire, that hissed and spluttered with his blood, and Lance Harriott with his smoking pistol, strode past him to the door. Already far down the trail there were hurried voices, the crack and crackling of impending branches growing fainter and fainter in the distance. Lance turned back to the solitary living figure — the old man.

Yet he might have been dead too, he sat so rigid and motionless, his fixed eyes staring vacantly at the body on the hearth. Before him on the table lay the cheap photographs, one evidently of himself, taken in some remote epoch of complexion, one of a child which Lance recognized as Flip.

"Tell me," said Lance hoarsely, laying his

quivering hand on the table, "was Bob Ridley your son?"

"My son," echoed the old man in a strange, far-off voice, without turning his eyes from the corpse — "My son — is — is — is there!" pointing to the dead man. "Hush! Did n't he tell you so? Didn't you hear him say it? Dead — dead — shot — shot!"

"Silence! are you crazy, man?" repeated Lance, tremblingly; "that is not Bob Ridley, but a dog, a coward, a liar gone to his reckoning. Hear me! If your son *was* Bob Ridley, I swear to God I never knew it, now or — or — *then*. Do you hear me? Tell me! Do you believe me? Speak! You shall speak."

He laid his hand almost menacingly on the old man's shoulder. Fairley slowly raised his head. Lance fell back with a groan of horror. The weak lips were wreathed with a feeble imploring smile, but the eyes wherein the fretful, peevish, suspicious spirit had dwelt were blank and tenantless; the flickering intellect that had lit them was blown out and vanished.

Lance walked toward the door and remained motionless for a moment, gazing into the night. When he turned back again toward the fire his face was as colorless as the dead man's on the hearth; the fire of passion was gone from his beaten eyes; his step was hesitating and slow. He went up to the table.

"I say, old man," he said, with a strange smile and an odd, premature suggestion of the infinite weariness of death in his voice, "you would n't mind giving me this, would you?" and he took up the picture of Flip. The old man nodded repeatedly. "Thank you," said Lance. He went to the door, paused a moment, and returned. "Good-by, old man," he said, holding out his hand. Fairley took it with a childish smile. "He's dead," said the old man softly, holding Lance's hand, but pointing to the hearth. "Yes," said Lance, with the faintest of smiles on the palest of faces. "You feel sorry for any one that's dead, don't you?" Fairley nodded again. Lance looked at him with eyes as remote as his own, shook his head, and turned away. When he reached the door he laid his revolver carefully, and, indeed, somewhat ostentatiously, upon a chair. But when he stepped from the threshold he stopped a moment in the light of the open door to examine the lock of a small derringer which he drew from his pocket. He then shut the door carefully, and with the same slow, hesitating step, felt his way into the night.

He had but one idea in his mind, to find some lonely spot; some spot where the footsteps of man would never penetrate, some spot that would yield him rest, sleep, obliteration, forgetfulness, and, above all, where *he* would be forgotten. He had seen such places; surely there were many, — where bones were picked up of dead men who had faded from the earth and had left no other record. If he could only keep his senses now he might find such a spot, but he must be careful, for her little feet went everywhere, and she must never see him again alive or dead. And in the midst of his thoughts, and the darkness, and the storm, he heard a voice at his side, " Lance, how long you have been ! "

. . . .

Left to himself, the old man again fell into a vacant contemplation of the dead body before him, until a stronger blast swept down like an avalanche upon the cabin, burst through the ill-fastened door and broken chimney, and, dashing the ashes and living embers over the floor, filled the room with blinding smoke and flame. Fairley rose with a feeble cry, and then, as if acted upon by some dominant memory, groped under the bed until he found his buckskin bag and his precious crystal, and fled precipitately from the room. Lifted by this second shock from his apathy, he returned to the fixed idea of his life, — the discovery and creation of the diamond, — and forgot all else. The feeble grasp that his shaken intellect kept of the events of the night relaxed, the disguised Lance, the story of his son, the murder, slipped into nothingness; there remained only the one idea, his nightly watch by the diamond pit. The instinct of long habit was stronger than the darkness or the onset of the storm, and he kept his tottering way over stream and fallen timber until he reached the spot. A sudden tremor seemed to shake the lambent flame that had lured him on. He thought he heard the sound of voices; there were signs of recent disturbance, — footprints in the sawdust! With a cry of rage and suspicion, Fairley slipped into the pit and sprang toward the nearest opening. To his frenzied fancy it had been tampered with, his secret discovered, the fruit of his long labors stolen from him that very night. With superhuman strength he began to open the pit, scattering the half-charred logs right and left, and giving vent to the suffocating gases that rose from the now incandescent charcoal. At times the fury of the gale would drive it back and hold it against the sides of the pit, leaving the opening free; at times, following the blind instinct of habit, the demented man would fall upon his face and bury his nose and mouth in the wet bark and sawdust. At last, the paroxysm past, he sank back again in his old apathetic attitude of watching, the attitude he had so often kept beside his sylvan crucible. In this attitude and in silence he waited for the dawn.

It came with a hush in the storm; it came with blue openings in the broken up and tumbled heavens; it came with stars that glistened first, and then paled, and at last sank drowning in those deep cerulean lakes; it came with those cerulean lakes broadening into vaster seas, whose shores expanded at last into one illimitable ocean, cerulean no more, but flecked with crimson and opal dyes; it came with the lightly lifted misty curtain of the day, torn and rent on crag and pine top, but always lifting, lifting. It came with the sparkle of emerald in the grasses, and the flash of diamonds in every spray, with a whisper in the awakening woods, and voices in the traveled roads and trails.

The sound of these voices stopped before the pit, and seemed to interrogate the old man. He came, and, putting his finger on his lips, made a sign of caution. When three or four men had descended he bade them follow him, saying, weakly and disjointedly, but persistently: "My boy — my son Robert — came home — came home at last — here with Flip — both of them — come and see!"

He had reached a little niche or nest in the hillside, and stopped and suddenly drew aside a blanket. Beneath it, side by side, lay Flip and Lance, dead, with their cold hands clasped in each other's.

"Suffocated!" said two or three, turning with horror toward the broken up and still smouldering pit.

"Asleep!" said the old man. "Asleep! I've seen 'em lying that way when they were babies together. Don't tell me! Don't say I don't know my own flesh and blood! So! so! So, my pretty ones!" He stooped and kissed them. Then, drawing the blanket over them gently, he rose and said softly, "Good night!"

FOUND AT BLAZING STAR.

FOUND AT BLAZING STAR.

THE rain had only ceased with the gray streaks of morning at Blazing Star, and the settlement awoke to a moral sense of cleanliness, and the finding of forgotten knives, tin cups, and smaller camp utensils, where the heavy showers had washed away the débris and dust heaps before the cabin doors. Indeed, it was recorded in Blazing Star that a fortunate early riser had once picked up on the highway a solid chunk of gold quartz which the rain had freed from its incumbering soil, and washed into immediate and glittering popularity. Possibly this may have been the reason why early risers in that locality, during the rainy season, adopted a thoughtful habit of body, and seldom lifted their eyes to the rifted or india-ink washed skies above them.

"Cass" Beard had risen early that morning, but not with a view to discovery. A leak in his cabin roof, — quite consistent with his careless, improvident habits, — had roused him at 4 A. M., with a flooded "bunk" and wet blankets. The chips from his wood pile refused to kindle a fire to dry his bed-clothes, and he had recourse to a more provident neighbor's to supply the deficiency. This was nearly opposite. Mr. Cassius crossed the highway, and stopped suddenly. Something glittered in the nearest red pool before him. Gold, surely! But, wonderful to relate, not an irregular, shapeless fragment of crude ore, fresh from Nature's crucible, but a bit of jeweler's handicraft in the form of a plain gold ring. Looking at it more attentively, he saw that it bore the inscription, "May to Cass."

Like most of his fellow gold-seekers, Cass was superstitious. "Cass!" His own name! He tried the ring. It fitted his little finger closely. It was evidently a woman's ring. He looked up and down the highway. No one was yet stirring. Little pools of water in the red road were beginning to glitter and grow rosy from the far-flushing east, but there was no trace of the owner of the shining waif. He knew that there was no woman in camp, and among his few comrades in the settlement he remembered to have seen none wearing an ornament like that. Again, the coincidence of the inscription to his rather peculiar nickname would have been a perennial source of playful comment in a camp that made no allowance for sentimental memories. He slipped the glittering little hoop into his pocket, and thoughtfully returned to his cabin.

Two hours later, when the long, straggling

procession, which every morning wended its way to Blazing Star Gulch, — the seat of mining operations in the settlement, — began to move, Cass saw fit to interrogate his fellows. " Ye did n't none on ye happen to drop anything round yer last night? " he asked, cautiously.

" I dropped a pocketbook containing government bonds and some other securities, with between fifty and sixty thousand dollars," responded Peter Drummond, carelessly; " but no matter, if any man will return a few autograph letters from foreign potentates that happened to be in it, — of no value to anybody but the owner, — he can keep the money. Thar 's nothin' mean about me," he concluded, languidly.

This statement, bearing every evidence of the grossest mendacity, was lightly passed over, and the men walked on with the deepest gravity.

"But hev you?" Cass presently asked of another.

"I lost my pile to Jack Hamlin at draw-poker, over at Wingdam last night," returned the other, pensively, "but I don't calkilate to find it lying round loose."

Forced at last by this kind of irony into more detailed explanation, Cass confided to them his discovery, and produced his treasure. The result was a dozen vague surmises, — only one of which seemed to be popular, and to suit the dyspeptic despondency of the party, — a despondency born of hastily masticated fried pork and flapjacks. The ring was believed to have been dropped by some passing "road agent" laden with guilty spoil.

"Ef I was you," said Drummond, gloomily, "I would n't flourish that yer ring around much afore folks. I've seen better men nor you strung up a tree by *Vigilantés* for having even less than that in their possession."

"And I would n't say much about bein' up so d—d early this morning," added an even more pessimistic comrade; "it might look bad before a jury."

With this the men sadly dispersed, leaving the innocent Cass with the ring in his hand, and a general impression on his mind that he was already an object of suspicion to his comrades,— an impression, it is hardly necessary to say, they fully intended should be left to rankle in his guileless bosom.

Notwithstanding Cass's first, hopeful superstition, the ring did not seem to bring him nor the camp any luck. Daily the "clean up" brought the same scant rewards to their labors, and deepened the sardonic gravity of Blazing Star. But, if Cass found no material result from his treasure, it stimulated his lazy imagination, and, albeit a dangerous and seductive stimulant, at least lifted him out of the monotonous grooves of his half-careless, half-slovenly, but always self-contented camp life. Heeding the wise caution of his comrades, he took the habit of wearing the ring only at night. Wrapped in his blanket, he stealthily slipped the golden circlet over his little finger, and, as he averred, " slept all the better for it." Whether it ever evoked any warmer dream or vision during those calm, cold, virgin-like spring nights, when even the moon and the greater planets retreated into the icy blue, steel-like firmament, I cannot say. Enough that this superstition began to be colored a little by fancy, and his fatalism somewhat mitigated by hope. Dreams of this kind did not tend to promote his efficiency in the communistic labors of the camp, and brought him a self-isolation that, however gratifying at first, soon debarred him the benefits of that hard practical wisdom which underlaid the grumbling of his fellow workers.

"I'm dog-goned," said one commentator,

"ef I don't believe that Cass is looney over that yer ring he found. Wears it on a string under his shirt."

Meantime, the seasons did not wait the discovery of the secret. The red pools in Blazing Star highway were soon dried up in the fervent June sun and riotous night winds of those altitudes. The ephemeral grasses that had quickly supplanted these pools and the chocolate-colored mud, were as quickly parched and withered. The footprints of spring became vague and indefinite, and were finally lost in the impalpable dust of the summer highway.

In one of his long, aimless excursions, Cass had penetrated a thick undergrowth of buckeye and hazel, and found himself quite unexpectedly upon the high road to Red Chief's Crossing. Cass knew by the lurid cloud of dust that hid the distance, that the up coach had passed. He had already reached that stage of superstition when the most trivial occurrence seemed to point in some way to an elucidation of the mystery of his treasure. His eyes had mechanically fallen to the ground again, as if he half expected to find in some other waif a hint or corroboration of his imaginings. Thus abstracted, the figure of a young girl on horseback, in the road directly before the bushes he emerged from, appeared to have sprung directly from the ground.

"Oh, come here, please do; quick!"

Cass stared, and then moved hesitatingly toward her.

"I heard some one coming through the bushes, and I waited," she went on. "Come quick. It's something too awful for anything."

In spite of this appalling introduction, Cass could not but notice that the voice, although hurried and excited, was by no means agitated or frightened; that the eyes which looked into his sparkled with a certain kind of pleased curiosity.

"It was just here," she went on vivaciously, "just here that I went into the bush and cut a switch for my mare, — and," — leading him along at a brisk trot by her side, — "just here, look, see! this is what I found."

It was scarcely thirty feet from the road. The only object that met Cass's eye was a man's stiff, tall hat, lying emptily and vacantly in the grass. It was new, shiny, and of modish shape. But it was so incongruous, so perkily smart, and yet so feeble and helpless lying there, so ghastly ludicrous in its very appropriateness and incapacity to adjust itself to the surrounding landscape, that it affected him with something more than a sense of its grotesqueness, and he could only stare at it blankly.

"But you're not looking the right way," the girl went on sharply; "look there!"

Cass followed the direction of her whip. At last, what might have seemed a coat thrown carelessly on the ground met his eye, but presently he became aware of a white, rigid, aimlessly-clinched hand protruding from the flaccid sleeve; mingled with it in some absurd way and half hidden by the grass, lay what might have been a pair of cast-off trousers but for two rigid boots that pointed in opposite angles to the sky. It was a dead man. So palpably dead that life seemed to have taken flight from his very clothes. So impotent, feeble, and degraded by them that the naked subject of a dissecting table would have been less insulting to humanity. The head had fallen back, and was partly hidden in a gopher burrow, but the white, upturned face and closed eyes had less of helpless death in them than those wretched enwrappings. Indeed, one limp hand that lay across the swollen abdomen lent itself to the grotesquely hideous suggestion of a gentleman sleeping off the excesses of a hearty dinner.

"Ain't he horrid?" continued the girl; "but what killed him?"

Struggling between a certain fascination at the girl's cold-blooded curiosity and horror of the murdered man, Cass hesitatingly lifted the helpless head. A bluish hole above the right temple, and a few brown paint-like spots on the forehead, shirt collar, and matted hair proved the only record.

"Turn him over again," said the girl, impatiently, as Cass was about to relinquish his burden. "May be you'll find another wound."

But Cass was dimly remembering certain formalities that in older civilizations attend the discovery of dead bodies, and postponed a present inquest.

"Perhaps you'd better ride on, Miss, afore you get summoned as a witness. I'll give warning at Red Chief's Crossing, and send the coroner down here."

"Let me go with you," she said, earnestly, "it would be such fun. I don't mind being a witness. Or," she added, without heeding Cass's look of astonishment, "I'll wait here till you come back."

"But you see, Miss, it would n't seem right,"— began Cass.

"But I found him first," interrupted the girl, with a pout.

Staggered by this preëmptive right, sacred to all miners, Cass stopped.

"Who is the coroner?" she asked.

"Joe Hornsby."

"The tall, lame man, who was half eaten by a grizzly?"

"Yes."

"Well, look now! I'll ride on and bring him back in half an hour. There!"

"But, Miss ——!"

"Oh, don't mind *me*. I never saw anything of this kind before, and I want to see it *all*."

"Do you know Hornsby?" asked Cass, unconsciously a trifle irritated.

"No, but I'll bring him." She wheeled her horse into the road.

In the presence of this living energy Cass quite forgot the helpless dead. "Have you been long in these parts, Miss?" he asked.

"About two weeks," she answered, shortly. "Good-by, just now. Look around for the pistol or anything else you can find, although *I* have been over the whole ground twice already."

A little puff of dust as the horse sprang into the road, a muffled shuffle, struggle, then the regular beat of hoofs, and she was gone.

After five minutes had passed, Cass regretted that he had not accompanied her: waiting in such a spot was an irksome task. Not that there was anything in the scene itself to awaken gloomy imaginings; the bright, truthful Californian sunshine scoffed at any illusion of creeping shadows or waving branches. Once, in the rising wind, the empty hat rolled over — but only in a ludicrous, drunken way. A search for any further sign or token had proved futile, and Cass grew impatient. He began to hate himself for having stayed; he would have fled but for shame. Nor was his good humor restored when at the close of a weary half hour two galloping figures emerged from the dusty horizon — Hornsby and the young girl.

His vague annoyance increased as he fancied that both seemed to ignore him, the coroner barely acknowledging his presence with a nod. Assisted by the young girl, whose energy and enthusiasm evidently delighted him, Hornsby raised the body for a more careful examination. The dead man's pockets were carefully searched. A few coins, a silver pencil, knife, and tobacco-box were all they found. It gave no clew to his identity. Suddenly the young girl, who had, with unabashed curiosity, knelt beside the exploring official hands of the Red Chief, uttered a cry of gratification.

"Here's something! It dropped from the bosom of his shirt on the ground. Look!"

She was holding in the air, between her thumb and forefinger, a folded bit of well-worn newspaper. Her eyes sparkled.

"Shall I open it?" she asked.

"Yes."

"It's a little ring," she said; "looks like an engagement ring. Something is written on it. Look! 'May to Cass.'"

Cass darted forward. "It's mine," he stammered, "mine! I dropped it. It's nothing — nothing," he went on, after a pause, embarrassed and blushing, as the girl and her companion both stared at him — "a mere trifle. I'll take it."

But the coroner opposed his outstretched hand. "Not much," he said, significantly.

"But it's *mine*," continued Cass, indignation taking the place of shame at his discovered secret. "I found it six months ago in the road. I — picked it up."

"With your name already written on it! How handy!" said the coroner, grimly.

"It's an old story," said Cass, blushing again under the half-mischievous, half-searching eyes of the girl. "All Blazing Star knows I found it."

"Then ye'll have no difficulty in provin' it," said Hornsby, coolly. "Just now, however, *we*'ve found it, and we propose to keep it for the inquest."

Cass shrugged his shoulders. Further altercation would have only heightened his ludicrous situation in the girl's eyes. He turned away, leaving his treasure in the coroner's hands.

The inquest, a day or two later, was prompt and final. No clew to the dead man's identity; no evidence sufficiently strong to prove murder or suicide; no trace of any kind, inculpating any party, known or unknown, were found. But much publicity and interest were given to the proceedings by the presence of the principal witness, a handsome girl. "To the pluck, persistency, and intellect of Miss Porter," said the "Red Chief Recorder," "Tuolumne County owes the recovery of the body."

No one who was present at the inquest failed to be charmed with the appearance and conduct of this beautiful young lady.

" Miss Porter has but lately arrived in this district, in which, it is hoped, she will become an honored resident, and continue to set an example to all lackadaisical and sentimental members of the so-called 'sterner sex.'" After this universally recognized allusion to Cass Beard, the "Recorder" returned to its record: "Some interest was excited by what appeared to be a clew to the mystery in the discovery of a small gold engagement ring on the body. Evidence was afterward offered to show it was the property of a Mr. Cass Beard of Blazing Star, who appeared upon the scene *after* the discovery of the corpse by Miss Porter. He alleged he had dropped it in lifting the unfortunate remains of the deceased. Much amusement was created in court by the sentimental confusion of the claimant, and a certain partisan spirit shown by his fellow-miners of Blazing Star. It appearing, however, by the admission of this sighing Strephon of the Foot Hills, that he had himself *found* this pledge of affection lying in the highway six months previous, the coroner wisely placed it in the safe-keeping of the county court until the appearance of the rightful owner."

Thus on the 13th of September, 186–, the treasure found at Blazing Star passed out of the hands of its finder.

. . . .

Autumn brought an abrupt explanation of the mystery. Kanaka Joe had been arrested for horse stealing, but had with noble candor confessed to the finer offense of manslaughter. That swift and sure justice which overtook the horse stealer in these altitudes was stayed a moment and hesitated, for the victim was clearly the mysterious unknown. Curiosity got the better of an extempore judge and jury.

"It was a fair fight," said the accused, not without some human vanity, feeling that the camp hung upon his words, "and was settled by the man az was peartest and liveliest with his weapon. We had a sort of unpleasantness over at Lagrange the night afore, along of our both hevin' a monotony of four aces. We had a clinch and a stamp around, and when we was separated it was only a question of shootin' on sight. He left Lagrange at sun up the next morning, and I struck across a bit o' buckeye and underbrush and came upon him, accidental like, on the Red Chief Road. I drawed when I sighted him, and called out. He slipped from his mare and covered himself with her flanks, reaching for his holster, but she rared and backed down on him across the road and into the grass, where I got in another shot and fetched him."

"And you stole his mare?" suggested the Judge.

"I got away," said the gambler, simply.

Further questioning only elicited the fact that Joe did not know the name or condition of his victim. He was a stranger in Lagrange.

It was a breezy afternoon, with some turbulency in the camp, and much windy discussion over this unwonted delay of justice. The suggestion that Joe should be first hung for horse stealing and then tried for murder was angrily discussed, but milder counsels were offered — that the fact of the killing should be admitted only as proof of the theft. A large party from Red Chief had come over to assist in judgment, among them the coroner.

Cass Beard had avoided these proceedings, which only recalled an unpleasant experience, and was wandering with pick, pan, and wallet far from the camp. These accoutrements, as I have before intimated, justified any form of aimless idleness under the equally aimless title of "prospecting." He had at the end of three hours' relaxation reached the highway to Red Chief, half hidden by blinding clouds of dust torn from the crumbling red road at every gust which swept down the mountain side. The spot had a familiar aspect to Cass, although some freshly-dug holes near the wayside, with scattered earth beside them, showed the presence of a recent prospector. He was struggling with his memory, when the dust was suddenly dispersed and he found himself again at the scene of the murder. He started: he had not put foot on the road since the inquest. There lacked only the helpless dead man and the contrasting figure of the alert young woman to restore the picture. The body was gone, it was true, but as he turned he beheld Miss Porter, at a few paces distant, sitting her horse as energetic and observant as on the first morning they had met. A superstitious thrill passed over him and awoke his old antagonism.

She nodded to him slightly. "I came here to refresh my memory," she said, "as Mr. Hornsby thought I might be asked to give my evidence again at Blazing Star."

Cass carelessly struck an aimless blow with his pick against the sod and did not reply.

"And you?" she queried.

"*I* stumbled upon the place just now while prospecting, or I shouldn't be here."

"Then it was *you* made these holes?"

"No," said Cass, with ill-concealed disgust. "Nobody but a stranger would go foolin' round such a spot."

He stopped, as the rude significance of his speech struck him, and added surlily. "I mean — no one would dig here."

The girl laughed and showed a set of very white teeth in her square jaw. Cass averted his face.

"Do you mean to say that every miner doesn't know that it's lucky to dig wherever human blood has been spilt?"

Cass felt a return of his superstition, but he did not look up. "I never heard it before," he said, severely.

"And you call yourself a California miner?"

"I do."

It was impossible for Miss Porter to misunderstand his curt speech and unsocial manner. She stared at him and colored slightly. Lifting her reins lightly, she said: "You certainly do not seem like most of the miners I have met."

"Nor you like any girl from the East I ever met," he responded.

"What do you mean?" she asked, checking her horse.

"What I say," he answered, doggedly. Reasonable as this reply was, it immediately struck him that it was scarcely dignified or manly. But before he could explain himself Miss Porter was gone.

He met her again that very evening. The trial had been summarily suspended by the appearance of the Sheriff of Calaveras and his *posse*, who took Joe from that self-constituted tribunal of Blazing Star and set his face southward and toward authoritative although more cautious justice. But not before the evidence of the previous inquest had been read, and the incident of the ring again delivered to the public. It is said the prisoner burst into an incredulous laugh and asked to see this mysterious waif. It was handed to him. Standing in the very shadow of the gallows tree — which might have been one of the pines that sheltered the billiard room in which the Vigilance Committee held their conclave — the prisoner gave way to a burst of merriment, so genuine and honest that the judge and jury joined in automatic sympathy. When silence was restored an explanation was asked by the Judge. But there was no response from the prisoner except a subdued chuckle.

"Did this ring belong to you?" asked the Judge, severely, the jury and spectators craning their ears forward with an expectant smile already on their faces. But the prisoner's eyes only sparkled maliciously as he looked around the court.

"Tell us, Joe," said a sympathetic and laughter-loving juror, under his breath. "Let it out and we'll make it easy for you."

"Prisoner," said the Judge, with a return of official dignity, "remember that your life is in peril. Do you refuse?"

Joe lazily laid his arm on the back of his chair with (to quote the words of an animated observer) "the air of having a Christian hope and a sequence flush in his hand," and said: "Well, as I reckon I'm not up yer for stealin' a ring that another man lets on to have found, and as fur as I kin see, hez nothin' to do with the case, I do!" And as it was here that the Sheriff of Calaveras made a precipitate entry into the room, the mystery remained unsolved.

The effect of this freshly-important ridicule on the sensitive mind of Cass might have been foretold by Blazing Star had it ever taken that sensitiveness into consideration. He had lost the good humor and easy pliability which had tempted him to frankness, and he had gradually become bitter and hard. He had at first affected amusement over his own vanished day dream — hiding his virgin disappointment in his own breast; but when he began to turn upon his feelings he turned upon his comrades also. Cass was for a while unpopular. There is no ingratitude so revolting to the human mind as that of the butt who refuses to be one any longer. The man who rejects that immunity which laughter generally casts upon him and demands to be seriously considered deserves no mercy.

It was under these hard conditions that Cass Beard, convicted of overt sentimentalism, aggravated by inconsistency, stepped into the Red Chief coach that evening. It was his habit usually to ride with the driver, but the presence of Hornsby and Miss Porter on the box seat changed his intention. Yet he had the satisfaction of seeing that neither had noticed him, and as there was no other passenger inside, he stretched himself on the cushion of the back seat and gave way to moody reflections. He quite determined to leave Blazing Star, to settle himself seriously to the task of money getting, and to return to his comrades, some day, a sarcastic, cynical, successful man, and so overwhelm them with confusion. For poor Cass had not yet reached that superiority of knowing that success would depend upon his ability to forego his past. Indeed, part of his boyhood had been cast among these men, and he was not old enough to have learned that success was not to be gauged by their standard. The moon lit up the dark interior of the coach with a faint poetic light. The lazy swinging of the vehicle that was bearing him away — albeit only for a night and a day —the solitude, the glimpses from the window of great distances full of vague possibilities, made the abused ring potent as that of Gyges. He dreamed with his eyes open. From an Alnaschar vision he suddenly awoke. The coach had stopped. The voices of men, one in entreaty, one in expostulation, came from the box. Cass mechanically put his hand to his pistol pocket.

"Thank you, but I *insist* upon getting down."

It was Miss Porter's voice. This was followed by a rapid, half-restrained interchange of words between Hornsby and the driver. Then the latter said, gruffly, —

"If the lady wants to ride inside, let her."

Miss Porter fluttered to the ground. She was followed by Hornsby. "Just a minit, Miss," he expostulated, half shamedly, half brusquely, "ye don't onderstand me. I only "—

But Miss Porter had jumped into the coach.

Hornsby placed his hand on the handle of the door. Miss Porter grasped it firmly from the inside. There was a slight struggle.

All of which was part of a dream to the boyish Cass. But he awoke from it — a man! "Do you," he asked, in a voice he scarcely recognized himself, — "Do you want this man inside?"

"No!"

Cass caught at Hornsby's wrist like a young tiger. But alas! what availed instinctive chivalry against main strength. He only succeeded in forcing the door open in spite of Miss Porter's superior strategy, and — I fear I must add, muscle also — and threw himself passionately at Hornsby's throat, where he hung on and calmly awaited dissolution. But he had, in the onset, driven Hornsby out into the road and the moonlight.

"Here! Somebody take my lines." The

voice was "Mountain Charley's," the driver. The figure that jumped from the box and separated the struggling men belonged to this singularly direct person.

"You're riding inside?" said Charley, interrogatively, to Cass. Before he could reply Miss Porter's voice came from the window.

"He is!"

Charley promptly bundled Cass into the coach.

"And *you?*" to Hornsby, "onless you're kalkilatin' to take a little 'pasear' you're booked *outside*. Get up."

It is probable that Charley assisted Mr. Hornsby as promptly to his seat, for the next moment the coach was rolling on.

Meanwhile Cass, by reason of his forced entry, had been deposited in Miss Porter's lap, whence, freeing himself, he had attempted to climb over the middle seat, but in the starting of the coach was again thrown heavily against her hat and shoulder; all of which was inconsistent with the attitude of dignified reserve he had intended to display. Miss Porter, meanwhile, recovered her good humor.

"What a brute he was, ugh!" she said, retying the ribbons of her bonnet under her square chin, and smoothing out her linen duster.

Cass tried to look as if he had forgotten the whole affair. "Who? Oh, yes! I see!" he responded, absently.

"I suppose I ought to thank you," she went on with a smile, "but you know, really, I could have kept him out if you had n't pulled his wrist from outside. I'll show you. Look! Put your hand on the handle there! Now, I'll hold the lock inside firmly. You see, you can't turn the catch!"

She indeed held the lock fast. It was a firm hand, yet soft — their fingers had touched over the handle — and looked white in the moonlight. He made no reply, but sank back again in his seat with a singular sensation in the fingers that had touched hers. He was in the shadow, and, without being seen, could abandon his reserve and glance at her face. It struck him that he had never really seen her before. She was not so tall as she had appeared to be. Her eyes were not large, but her pupils were black, moist, velvety, and so convex as to seem embossed on the white. She had an indistinctive nose, a rather colorless face — whiter at the angles of the mouth and nose through the relief of tiny freckles like grains of pepper. Her mouth was straight, dark, red, but moist as her eyes. She had drawn herself into the corner of the back seat, her wrist put through and hanging over the swinging strap, the easy lines of her plump figure swaying from side to side with the motion of the coach. Finally, forgetful of any presence in the dark corner opposite, she threw her head a little farther back, slipped a trifle lower, and placing two well-booted feet upon the middle seat, completed a charming and wholesome picture.

Five minutes elapsed. She was looking straight at the moon. Cass Beard felt his dignified reserve becoming very much like awkwardness. He ought to be coldly polite.

"I hope you're not flustered, Miss, by the — by the"— he began.

"I?" She straightened herself up in the seat, cast a curious glance into the dark corner, and then, letting herself down again, said: "Oh, dear, no!"

Another five minutes elapsed. She had evidently forgotten him. She might, at least, have been civil. He took refuge again in his reserve. But it was now mixed with a certain pique.

Yet how much softer her face looked in the moonlight! Even her square jaw had lost that hard, matter-of-fact, practical indication which was so distasteful to him, and always had suggested a harsh criticism of his weakness. How moist her eyes were — actually shining in the light! How that light seemed to concentrate in the corner of the lashes, and then slipped — a flash — away! Was she? Yes, she was crying.

Cass melted. He moved. Miss Porter put her head out of the window and drew it back in a moment, dry-eyed.

"One meets all sorts of folks traveling," said Cass, with what he wished to make appear a cheerful philosophy.

"I dare say. I don't know. I never before met any one who was rude to me. I have traveled all over the country alone, and with all kinds of people ever since I was so high. I have always gone my own way, without hindrance or trouble. I always do. I don't see why I should n't. Perhaps other people may n't like it. I do. I like excitement. I like to see all that there is to see. Because I 'm a girl I don't see why I cannot go out without a keeper, and why I cannot do what any man can do that is n't wrong, do you? Perhaps you do — perhaps you don't. Perhaps you like a girl to be always in the house dawdling or thumping a piano or reading novels. Perhaps you think I 'm bold because I don't like it, and won't lie and say I do."

She spoke sharply and aggressively, and so evidently in answer to Cass's unspoken indictment against her, that he was not surprised when she became more direct.

"You know you were shocked when I went to fetch that Hornsby, the coroner, after we found the dead body."

"Hornsby was n't shocked," said Cass, a little viciously.

"What do you mean?" she said, abruptly.

"You were good friends enough until"—

"Until he insulted me just now, is that it?"

"Until he thought," stammered Cass, "that because you were — you know — not so — so — so careful as other girls, he could be a little freer."

"And so, because I preferred to ride a mile with him to see something real that had happened, and tried to be useful instead of looking in shop windows in Main Street or promenading before the hotel"—

"And being ornamental," interrupted Cass. But this feeble and un-Cass-like attempt at playful gallantry met with a sudden check.

Miss Porter drew herself together, and looked out of the window. "Do you wish me to walk the rest of the way home?"

"No," said Cass, hurriedly, with a crimson face and a sense of gratuitous rudeness.

"Then stop that kind of talk, right there!"

There was an awkward silence. "I wish I

was a man," she said, half bitterly, half earnestly. Cass Beard was not old and cynical enough to observe that this devout aspiration is usually uttered by those who have least reason to deplore their own femininity; and, but for the rebuff he had just received, would have made the usual emphatic dissent of our sex, when the wish is uttered by warm red lips and tender voices — a dissent, it may be remarked, generally withheld, however, when the masculine spinster dwells on the perfection of woman. I dare say Miss Porter was sincere, for a moment later she continued, poutingly:

"And yet I used to go to fires in Sacramento when I was only ten years old. I saw the theatre burnt down. Nobody found fault with me then."

Something made Cass ask if her father and mother objected to her boyish tastes. The reply was characteristic if not satisfactory, —

"Object? I'd like to see them do it."

The direction of the road had changed. The fickle moon now abandoned Miss Porter and sought out Cass on the front seat. It caressed the young fellow's silky moustache and long eyelashes, and took some of the sunburn from his cheek.

"What's the matter with your neck?" said the girl, suddenly.

Cass looked down, blushing to find that the collar of his smart "duck" sailor shirt was torn open. But something more than his white, soft, girlish skin was exposed; the shirt front was dyed quite red with blood from a slight cut on the shoulder. He remembered to have felt a scratch while struggling with Hornsby.

The girl's soft eyes sparkled. "Let *me*," she said, vivaciously. "Do! I'm good at wounds. Come over here. No — stay there. I'll come over to you."

She did, bestriding the back of the middle

seat and dropping at his side. The magnetic fingers again touched his; he felt her warm breath on his neck as she bent toward him.

"It's nothing," he said, hastily, more agitated by the treatment than the wound.

"Give me your flask," she responded, without heeding. A stinging sensation as she bathed the edges of the cut with the spirit brought him back to common sense again. "There," she said, skillfully extemporizing a bandage from her handkerchief and a compress from his cravat. "Now, button your coat over your chest, so, and don't take cold." She insisted upon buttoning it for him; greater even than the feminine delight in a man's strength is the ministration to his weakness. Yet, when this was finished, she drew a little away from him in some embarrassment — an embarrassment she wondered at, as his skin was finer, his touch gentler, his clothes cleaner, and — not to put too fine a point upon it — he exhaled an atmosphere much sweeter than belonged to most of the men her boyish habits had brought her in contact with — not excepting her own father. Later she even exempted her mother from the possession of this divine effluence. After moment she asked, suddenly, "What are you going to do with Hornsby?"

Cass had not thought of him. His short-lived rage was past with the occasion that provoked it. Without any fear of his adversary he would have been content quite willing to meet him no more. He only said, "That will depend upon him."

"Oh, you won't hear from him again," said she, confidently, "but you really ought to get up a little more muscle. You've no more than a girl." She stopped, a little confused.

"What shall I do with your handkerchief?" asked the uneasy Cass, anxious to change the subject.

"Oh, keep it, if you want to, only don't show it to everybody as you did that ring you found." Seeing signs of distress in his face, she added: "Of course that was all nonsense. If you had cared so much for the ring you could n't have talked about it, or shown it. Could you?"

It relieved him to think that this might be true; he certainly had not looked at it in that light before.

"But did you really find it?" she asked, with sudden gravity. "Really, now?"

"Yes."

"And there was no real May in the case?"

"Not that I know of," laughed Cass, secretly pleased.

But Miss Porter, after eying him critically for a moment, jumped up and climbed back again to her seat. "Perhaps you had better give me that handkerchief back."

Cass began to unbutton his coat.

"No! no! Do you want to take your death of cold?" she screamed. And Cass, to avoid this direful possibility, rebuttoned his coat again over the handkerchief and a peculiarly pleasing sensation.

Very little now was said until the rattling, bounding descent of the coach denoted the approach to Red Chief. The straggling main street disclosed itself, light by light. In the flash of glittering windows and the sound of eager voices Miss Porter descended, without waiting for Cass's proffered assistance, and anticipated Mountain Charley's descent from the box. A few undistinguishable words passed between them.

"You kin freeze to me, Miss," said Charley; and Miss Porter, turning her frank laugh and frankly opened palm to Cass, half returned the pressure of his hand and slipped away.

A few days after the stage coach incident,

Mountain Charley drew up beside Cass on the Blazing Star turnpike, and handed him a small packet. "I was told to give ye that by Miss Porter. Hush — listen! It's that rather old dog-goned ring o' yours that's bin in all the papers. She's bamboozled that sap-headed county judge, Boompointer, into givin' it to her. Take my advice and sling it away for some other feller to pick up and get looney over. That's all!"

"Did she say anything?" asked Cass, anxiously, as he received his lost treasure somewhat coldly.

"Well, yes! I reckon. She asked me to stand betwixt Hornsby and you. So don't *you* tackle him, and I'll see *he* don't tackle you," and with a portentous wink Mountain Charley whipped up his horses and was gone.

Cass opened the packet. It contained nothing but the ring. Unmitigated by any word of greeting, remembrance, or even railery, it seemed almost an insult. Had she intended to flaunt his folly in his face, or had she believed he still mourned for it and deemed its recovery a sufficient reward for his slight service? For an instant he felt tempted to follow Charley's advice, and cast this symbol of folly and contempt in the dust of the mountain road. And had she not made his humiliation complete by begging Charley's interference between him and his enemy? He would go home and send her back the handkerchief she had given him. But here the unromantic reflection that although he had washed it that very afternoon in the solitude of his own cabin, he could not possibly iron it, but must send it " rough dried," stayed his indignant feet.

Two or three days, a week, a fortnight even, of this hopeless resentment filled Cass's breast. Then the news of Kanaka Joe's acquittal in the State Court momentarily revived the story of the ring, and revamped a few stale jokes in the camp. But the interest soon flagged; the fortunes of the little community of Blazing Star had been for some months failing; and with early snows in the mountain and wasted capital in fruitless schemes on the river, there was little room for the indulgence of that lazy and original humor which belonged to their lost youth and prosperity. Blazing Star truly, in the grim figure of their slang, was " played out." Not dug out, worked out, or washed out, but dissipated in a year of speculation and chance.

Against this tide of fortune Cass struggled manfully, and even evoked the slow praise of his companions. Better still, he won a certain praise for himself, in himself, in a consciousness of increased strength, health, power, and self-reliance. He began to turn his quick imagination and perception to some practical account, and made one or two discoveries which quite startled his more experienced, but more conservative companions. Nevertheless, Cass's discoveries and labors were not of a kind that produced immediate pecuniary realization, and Blazing Star, which consumed so many pounds of pork and flour daily, did not unfortunately produce the daily equivalent in gold. Blazing Star lost its credit. Blazing Star was hungry, dirty, and ragged. Blazing Star was beginning to set.

Participating in the general ill luck of the camp, Cass was not without his own individual mischances. He had resolutely determined to forget Miss Porter and all that tended to recall the unlucky ring, but, cruelly enough, she was the only thing that refused to be forgotten — whose undulating figure reclined opposite to him in the weird moonlight of his ruined cabin, whose voice mingled with the song of the river by whose banks he toiled, and whose eyes and touch thrilled him in his dreams. Partly for this reason, and partly because his clothes were beginning to be patched and torn, he avoided Red Chief and any place where he would be likely to meet her. In spite of this precaution he had once seen her driving in a pony carriage, but so smartly and fashionably dressed that he drew back in the cover of a wayside willow that she might pass without recognition. He looked down upon his red-splashed clothes and grimy, soil-streaked hands, and for a moment half hated her. His comrades seldom spoke of her — instinctively fearing some temptation that might beset his Spartan resolutions, but he heard from time to time that she had been seen at balls and parties, apparently enjoying those very frivolities of her sex she affected to condemn. It was a Sabbath morning in early spring that he was returning from an ineffectual attempt to enlist a capitalist at the county town to redeem the fortunes of Blazing Star. He was pondering over the narrowness of that capitalist, who had evidently but illogically connected Cass's present appearance with the future of that struggling camp, when he became so footsore that he was obliged to accept a "lift" from a wayfaring teamster. As the slowly lumbering vehicle passed the new church on the outskirts of the town, the congregation were sallying forth. It was too late to jump down and run away, and Cass dared not ask his new-found friend to whip up his cattle. Conscious of his unshorn beard and ragged garments, he kept his eyes fixed upon the road. A voice that thrilled him called his name. It was Miss Porter, a resplendent vision of silk, laces, and Easter flowers — yet actually running, with something of her old dash and freedom, beside the wagon. As the astonished teamster drew up before this elegant apparition, she panted: —

"Why did you make me run so far, and why did n't you look up?"

Cass, trying to hide the patches on his knees beneath a newspaper, stammered that he had not seen her.

"And you did not hold down your head purposely?"

"No," said Cass.

"Why have you not been to Red Chief? Why did n't you answer my message about the ring?" she asked, swiftly.

"You sent nothing but the ring," said Cass, coloring, as he glanced at the teamster.

"Why, *that* was a message, you born idiot."

Cass stared. The teamster smiled. Miss Porter gazed anxiously at the wagon. "I think I 'd like a ride in there; it looks awfully good." She glanced mischievously around at the lingering and curious congregation. "May I?"

But Cass deprecated that proceeding strongly. It was dirty; he was not sure it was even *wholesome;* she would be *so* uncomfortable; he, himself, was only going a few rods farther, and in that time she might ruin her dress —

"Oh, yes," she said, a little bitterly, "certainly, my dress must be looked after. And — what else?"

"People might think it strange, and believe I had invited you," continued Cass, hesitatingly.

"When I had only invited myself? Thank you. Good-by."

She waved her hand and stepped back from the wagon. Cass would have given worlds to recall her, but he sat still, and the vehicle moved on in moody silence. At the first cross road he jumped down. "Thank you," he said to the teamster. "You're welcome," returned that gentleman, regarding him curiously, "but the next time a gal like that asks to ride in this yer wagon, I reckon I won't take the vote of any deadhead passenger. *Adios*, young fellow. Don't stay out late; ye might be run off by some gal, and what would your mother say?" Of course the young man could only look unutterable things and walk away, but even in that dignified action he was conscious that its effect was somewhat mitigated by a large patch from a material originally used as a flour sack, which had repaired his trousers, but still bore the ironical legend, " Best Superfine."

The summer brought warmth and promise and some blossom, if not absolute fruition to Blazing Star. The long days drew Nature into closer communion with the men, and hopefulness followed the discontent of their winter seclusion. It was easier, too, for Capital to be wooed and won into making a picnic in these mountain solitudes than when high water stayed the fords and drifting snow the

Sierran trails. At the close of one of these Arcadian days Cass was smoking before the door of his lonely cabin when he was astounded by the onset of a dozen of his companions. Peter Drummond, far in the van, was waving a newspaper like a victorious banner. "All's right now, Cass, old man!" he panted as he stopped before Cass and shoved back his eager followers.

"What's all right?" asked Cass, dubiously.

You! You kin rake down the pile now. You're hunky! You're on velvet. Listen!"

He opened the newspaper and read, with annoying deliberation, as follows: —

"LOST. — If the finder of a plain gold ring, bearing the engraved inscription, 'May to Cass,' alleged to have been picked up on the high road near Blazing Star on the 4th March, 186-, will apply to Bookham & Sons, bankers, 1007 Y. Street, Sacramento, he will be suitably rewarded either for the recovery of the ring, or for such facts as may identify it, or the locality where it was found."

Cass rose and frowned savagely on his comrades. "No! no!" cried a dozen voices, assuringly. "It's all right! Honest Injun! True as gospel! No joke, Cass!"

"Here's the paper, Sacramento "Union" of yesterday. Look for yourself," said Drummond, handing him the well-worn journal. "And you see," he added, "how darned lucky you are. It ain't necessary for you to produce the ring, so if that old biled owl of a Boompointer don't giv' it back to ye, it's all the same."

"And they say nobody but the finder need apply," interrupted another. "That shuts out Boompointer or Kanaka Joe for the matter o' that."

"It's clar that it *means* you, Cass, ez much ez if they'd given your name," added a third.

For Miss Porter's sake and his own Cass

had never told them of the restoration of the ring, and it was evident that Mountain Charley had also kept silent. Cass could not speak now without violating a secret, and he was pleased that the ring itself no longer played an important part in the mystery. But what was that mystery, and why was the ring secondary to himself? Why was so much stress laid upon his finding it?

"You see," said Drummond, as if answering his unspoken thought, 'that 'ar gal — for it is a gal in course — hez read all about it in the papers, and hez sort o' took a shine to ye. It don't make a bit o' difference who in thunder Cass *is* or *waz*, for I reckon she's kicked him over by this time" —

"Sarved him right, too, for losing the girl's ring and then lying low and keeping dark about it," interrupted a sympathizer.

"And she's just weakened over the romantic, high-toned way you stuck to it," continued

Drummond, forgetting the sarcasms he had previously hurled at this romance. Indeed the whole camp, by this time, had become convinced that it had fostered and developed a chivalrous devotion which was now on the point of pecuniary realization. It was generally accepted that "she" was the daughter of this banker, and also felt that in the circumstances the happy father could not do less than develop the resources of Blazing Star at once. Even if there were no relationship, what opportunity could be more fit for presenting to capital a locality that even produced engagement rings, and, as Jim Fauquier put it, "the men ez knew how to keep 'em." It was this sympathetic Virginian who took Cass aside with the following generous suggestion: "If you find that you and the old gal couldn't hitch hosses, owin' to your not likin' red hair or a game leg" (it may be here recorded that Blazing Star had, for no reason whatever, attributed these unprepossessing qualities to the mysterious advertiser), " you might let *me* in. You might say ez how I used to jest worship that ring with you, and allers wanted to borrow it on Sundays. If anything comes of it — why — *we're pardners!*"

A serious question was the outfitting of Cass for what now was felt to be a diplomatic representation of the community. His garments, it hardly need be said, were inappropriate to any wooing except that of the " maiden all forlorn," which the advertiser clearly was not. " He might," suggested Fauquier, " drop in jest as he is — kinder as if he 'd got keerless of the world, being lovesick." But Cass objected strongly, and was borne out in his objection by his younger comrades. At last a pair of white duck trousers, a red shirt, a flowing black silk scarf, and a Panama hat were procured at Red Chief, on credit, after a judicious exhibition of the advertisement. A heavy wedding ring, the property of Drummond (who was not married), was also lent as a graceful suggestion, and at the last moment Fauquier affixed to Cass's scarf an enormous specimen pin of gold and quartz. "It sorter indicates the auriferous wealth o' this yer region, and the old man (the senior member of Bookham & Sons) need n't know I won it at draw poker in Frisco," said Fauqier.

"Ef you 'pass' on the gal, you kin hand it back to me and *I'll* try it on." Forty dollars for expenses was put into Cass's hands, and the entire community accompanied him to the cross roads where he was to meet the Sacramento coach, which eventually carried him away, followed by a benediction of waving hats and exploding revolvers.

That Cass did not participate in the extravagant hopes of his comrades, and that he rejected utterly their matrimonial speculations in his behalf, need not be said. Outwardly, he kept his own counsel with good-humored assent. But there was something fascinating in the situation, and while he felt he had forever abandoned his romantic dream, he was not displeased to know that it might have proved a reality. Nor was it distasteful to him to think that Miss Porter would hear of it and regret her late inability to appreciate his sentiment. If he really were the object of some opulent maiden's passion, he would show Miss Porter how he could sacrifice the most brilliant prospects for her sake. Alone, on the top of the coach, he projected one of those satisfying conversations in which imaginative people delight, but which unfortunately never come quite up to rehearsal. "Dear Miss Porter," he would say, addressing the back of the driver, "if I could remain faithful to a dream of my youth, however illusive and unreal, can you believe that for the sake of lucre I could be false to the one real passion that alone supplanted it." In the composition and delivery of this eloquent statement an hour was happily forgotten: the only drawback to its complete effect was that a misplace of epithets in rapid repetition did not seem to make the slightest difference, and Cass found himself saying "Dear Miss Porter, if I could be false to a dream of my youth, etc., etc., can you believe I could be *faithful* to the one real passion, etc., etc.," with equal and perfect satisfaction. As Miss Porter was reputed to be well off, if the unknown were poor, that might be another drawback.

The banking house of Bookham & Sons did not present an illusive nor mysterious appearance. It was eminently practical and matter of fact; it was obtrusively open and glassy; nobody would have thought of leaving a secret there that would have been inevitaby circulated over the counter. Cass felt an uncomfortable sense of incongruity in himself, in his story, in his treasure, to this temple of disenchanting realism. With the awkwardness of an embarrassed man he was holding prominently in his hand an envelope containing the ring and advertisement as a voucher for his intrusion, when the nearest clerk took the envelope from his hand, opened it, took out the ring, returned it, said briskly, " T' other shop, next door, young man," and turned to another customer.

Cass stepped to the door, saw that " T' other shop" was a pawnbroker's, and returned again with a flashing eye and heightened color. " It's an advertisement I have come to answer," he began again.

The clerk cast a glance at Cass's scarf and pin. " Place taken yesterday — no room for any more," he said, abruptly.

Cass grew quite white. But his old experience in Blazing Star repartee stood him in good stead. "If it's *your* place you mean," he said coolly, "I reckon you might put a dozen men in the hole you're rattlin' round in — but it's this advertisement I'm after. If Bookham isn't in, maybe you'll send me one of the grown-up sons." The production of the advertisement and some laughter from the bystanders had its effect. The pert young clerk retired, and returned to lead the way to the bank parlor. Cass's heart sank again as he was confronted by a dark, iron-gray man — in dress, features, speech, and action — uncompromisingly opposed to Cass — his ring and his romance. When the young man had told his story and produced his treasure he paused. The banker scarcely glanced at it, but said, impatiently, —

"Well, your papers?"

"My papers?"

"Yes. Proof of your identity. You say

your name is Cass Beard. Good! What have you got to prove it? How can I tell who you are?"

To a sensitive man there is no form of suspicion that is as bewildering and demoralizing at the moment as the question of his identity. Cass felt the insult in the doubt of his word, and the palpable sense of his present inability to prove it. The banker watched him keenly but not unkindly.

"Come," he said at length, "this is not my affair; if you can legally satisfy the lady for whom I am only agent, well and good. I believe you can; I only warn you that you must. And my present inquiry was to keep her from losing her time with imposters, a class I don't think you belong to. There's her card. Good day."

"Miss Mortimer." It was *not* the banker's daughter. The first illusion of Blazing Star was rudely dispelled. But the care taken by the capitalist to shield her from imposture indicated a person of wealth. Of her youth and beauty Cass no longer thought.

The address given was not distant. With a beating heart he rung the bell of a respectable-looking house, and was ushered into a private drawing-room. Instinctively he felt that the room was only temporarily inhabited; an air peculiar to the best lodgings, and when the door opened upon a tall lady in deep mourning, he was still more convinced of an incongruity between the occupant and her surroundings. With a smile that vacillated between a habit of familiarity and ease, and a recent restraint, she motioned him to a chair.

"Miss Mortimer" was still young, still handsome, still fashionably dressed, and still attractive. From her first greeting to the end of the interview Cass felt that she knew all about him. This relieved him from the onus of proving his identity, but seemed to put him vaguely at a disadvantage. It increased his sense of inexperience and youthfulness.

"I hope you will believe," she began, "that the few questions I have to ask you are to satisfy my own heart, and for no other purpose." She smiled sadly as she went on. "Had it been otherwise, I should have instituted a legal inquiry, and left this interview to some one cooler, calmer, and less interested than myself. But I think, I *know* I can trust you. Perhaps we women are weak and foolish to talk of an *instinct*, and when you know my story you may have reason to believe that but little dependence can be placed on *that*; but I am not wrong in saying, — am I?" (with a sad smile) "that *you* are not above that weakness?" She paused, closed her lips tightly, and grasped her hands before her. "You say you found that ring in the road some three months before — the — the — you know what I mean — the body — was discovered?"

"Yes."

"You thought it might have been dropped by some one in passing?"

"I thought so, yes — it belonged to no one in camp."

"Before your cabin or on the highway?"

"Before my cabin."

"You are *sure?*" There was something so very sweet and sad in her smile that it oddly made Cass color.

"But my cabin is near the road," he suggested.

"I see! And there was nothing else; no paper nor envelope?"

"Nothing."

"And you kept it because of the odd resemblance one of the names bore to yours?"

"Yes."

"For no other reason?"

"None." Yet Cass felt he was blushing.

"You'll forgive my repeating a question you have already answered, but I am *so* anxious. There was some attempt to prove at the inquest that the ring had been found on the body of — the unfortunate man. But you tell me it was not so?"

"I can swear it."

"Good God — the traitor!" She took a hurried step forward, turned to the window, and then came back to Cass with a voice broken with emotion. "I have told you I could trust you. That ring was mine!"

She stopped, and then went on hurriedly. "Years ago I gave it to a man who deceived and wronged me; a man whose life since then has been a shame and disgrace to all who knew him. A man who, once, a gentleman, sank so low as to become the associate of thieves and ruffians; sank so low, that when he died, by violence — a traitor even to them

— his own confederates shrunk from him, and left him to fill a nameless grave. That man's body you found!"

Cass started. "And his name was——?"

"Part of your surname. Cass — Henry Cass."

"You see why Providence seems to have brought that ring to you," she went on. "But you ask me why, knowing this, I am so eager to know if the ring was found by you in the road, or if it were found on his body. Listen! It is part of my mortification that the story goes that this man once showed this ring, boasted of it, staked, and lost it at a gambling table to one of his vile comrades."

"Kanaka Joe," said Cass, overcome by a vivid recollection of Joe's merriment at the trial.

"The same. Don't you see," she said, hurriedly, "if the ring had been found on him I could believe that somewhere in his heart he still kept respect for the woman he had wronged. I am a woman — a foolish woman, I know — but you have crushed that hope forever."

"But why have you sent for me?" asked Cass, touched by her emotion.

"To know it for certain," she said, almost fiercely. "Can you not understand that a woman like me must know a thing once and forever? But you *can* help me. I did not send for you only to pour my wrongs in your ears. You must take me with you to this place — to the spot where you found the ring — to the spot where you found the body — to the spot where — where *he* lies. You must do it secretly, that none shall know me."

Cass hesitated. He was thinking of his companions and the collapse of their painted bubble. How could he keep the secret from them?

"If it is money you need, let not that

stop you. I have no right to your time without recompense. Do not misunderstand me. There has been a thousand dollars awaiting my order at Bookham's when the ring should be delivered. It shall be doubled if you help me in this last moment."

It was possible. He could convey her secretly there, invent some story of a reward delayed for want of proofs, and afterward share that reward with his friends. He answered promptly, "I will take you there."

She took his hands in both of hers, raised them to her lips, and smiled. The shadow of grief and restraint seemed to have fallen from her face, and a half-mischievous, half-coquettish gleam in her dark eyes touched the susceptible Cass in so subtle a fashion that he regained the street in some confusion. He wondered what Miss Porter would have thought. But was he not returning to her, a fortunate man, with one thousand dollars in his pocket! Why should he remember he was handicapped, by a pretty woman and a pathetic episode? It did not make the proximity less pleasant as he helped her into the coach that evening, nor did the recollection of another ride with another woman obtrude itself upon those consolations which he felt it his duty, from time to time, to offer. It was arranged that he should leave her at the " Red Chief " Hotel, while he continued on to Blazing Star, returning at noon to bring her with him when he could do it without exposing her to recognition. The gray dawn came soon enough, and the coach drew up at " Red Chief " while the lights in the bar-room and dining-room of the hotel were still struggling with the far flushing east. Cass alighted, placed Miss Mortimer in the hands of the landlady, and returned to the vehicle. It was still musty, close, and frowzy, with half-awakened passengers. There was a vacated seat on the top, which Cass climbed up to, and abstractedly threw himself beside a figure muffled in shawls and rugs. There was a slight movement among the multitudinous enwrappings, and then the figure turned to him and said, dryly, "Good morning!" It was Miss Porter!

"Have you been long here?" he stammered.

"All night."

He would have given worlds to leave her at that moment. He would have jumped from the starting coach to save himself any explanation of the embarrassment he was furiously conscious of showing, without, as he believed, any adequate cause. And yet, like all inexperienced, sensitive men, he dashed blindly into that explanation; worse, he even told his secret at once, then and there, and then sat abashed and conscience stricken, with an added sense of its utter futility.

"And this," summed up the young girl, with a slight shrug of her pretty shoulders, "is *your May?*"

Cass would have recommenced his story.

"No, don't, pray! It is n't interesting, nor original. Do *you* believe it?"

"I do," said Cass, indignantly.

"How lucky! Then let me go to sleep."

Cass, still furious, but uneasy, did not again address her. When the coach stopped at Blazing Star she asked him, indifferently: "When does this sentimental pilgrimage begin?"

"I return for her at one o'clock," replied Cass, stiffly.

He kept his word. He appeased his eager companions with a promise of future fortune, and exhibited the present and tangible reward. By a circuitous route known only to himself, he led Miss Mortimer to the road before the cabin. There was a pink flush of excitement on her somewhat faded cheek.

"And it was here?" she asked, eagerly.

"I found it here."

"And the body?"

"That was afterward. Over in that direction, beyond the clump of buckeyes, on the Red Chief turnpike."

"And any one coming from the road we left just now and going to — to — that place, would have to cross just here? Tell me," she said, with a strange laugh, laying her cold nervous hand on his, "would n't they?"

"They would."

"Let us go to that place."

Cass stepped out briskly to avoid observation and gain the woods beyond the highway. "You have crossed here before," she said. "There seems to be a trail."

"I may have made it: it's a short cut to the buckeyes."

"You never found anything else on the trail?"

"You remember, I told you before, the ring was all I found."

"Ah, true!" she smiled sweetly; "it was *that* which made it seem so odd to you. I forgot."

In half an hour they reached the buckeyes. During the walk she had taken rapid recognizance of everything in her path. When they crossed the road and Cass had pointed out the scene of the murder, she looked anxiously around. "You are sure we are not seen?"

"Quite."

"You will not think me foolish if I ask you to wait here while I go in there" — she pointed to the ominous thicket near them — "alone?" She was quite white.

Cass's heart, which had grown somewhat cold since his interview with Miss Porter, melted at once.

"Go; I will stay here."

He waited five minutes. She did not return. What if the poor creature had determined upon suicide on the spot where her faithless lover had fallen? He was reassured in another moment by the rustle of skirts in the undergrowth.

"I was becoming quite alarmed," he said, aloud.

"You have reason to be," returned a hurried voice. He started. It was Miss Porter, who stepped swiftly out of the cover. "Look," she said, "look at that man down the road. He has been tracking you two ever since you left the cabin. Do you know who he is?"

"No!"

"Then listen. It is three-fingered Dick, one of the escaped road agents. I know him!"

"Let us go and warn her," said Cass, eagerly.

Miss Porter laid her hand upon his shoulder.

"I don't think she'll thank you," she said, dryly. " Perhaps you'd better see what she's doing, first.

Utterly bewildered, yet with a strong sense of the masterfulness of his companion, he followed her. She crept like a cat through the thicket. Suddenly she paused. "Look!" she whispered, viciously, "look at the tender vigils of your heart-broken May!"

Cass saw the woman who had left him a moment before on her knees on the grass, with long thin fingers digging like a ghoul in the earth. He had scarce time to notice her eager face and eyes, cast now and then back toward the spot where she had left him, before there was a crash in the bushes, and a man, — the stranger of the road, — leaped to her side. "Run," he said; "run for it now. You're watched!"

"Oh! that man, Beard!" she said, contemptuously.

"No, another in a wagon. Quick. Fool, you know the place now, — you can come later; run!" And half-dragging, half-lifting her, he bore her through the bushes. Scarcely had they closed behind the pair than Miss Porter ran to the spot vacated by the woman. "Look!" she cried, triumphantly, "look!".

Cass looked, and sank on his knees beside her.

"It *was* worth a thousand dollars, was n't it?" she repeated, maliciously, "was n't it? But you ought to return it! *Really* you ought."

Cass could scarcely articulate. "But how did *you* know it?" he finally gasped.

"Oh, I suspected something; there was a woman, and you know you 're *such* a fool!"

Cass rose, stiffly.

"Don't be a greater fool now, but go and bring my horse and wagon from the hill, and don't say anything to the driver."

"Then you did not come alone?"

"No; it would have been bold and improper."

"Please!"

"And to think it *was* the ring, after all, that pointed to this," she said.

"The ring that *you* returned to me."

"What did you say?"

"Nothing."

"Don't, please, the wagon is coming."

. . . .

In the next morning's edition of the "Red Chief Chronicle" appeared the following startling intelligence: —

EXTRAORDINARY DISCOVERY

FINDING OF THE STOLEN TREASURE OF WELLS, FARGO & CO. OVER $300,000 RECOVERED.

Our readers will remember the notorious robbery of Wells, Fargo & Co.'s treasure from the Sacramento and Red Chief Pioneer Coach on the night of September 1. Although most of the gang were arrested, it is known that two escaped, who, it was presumed, *cached* the treasure, amounting to nearly $500,000 in gold, drafts, and jewelry, as no trace of the property was found. Yesterday our esteemed fellow citizen, Mr. Cass Beard, long and favorably known in this county, succeeded in exhuming the treasure in a copse of hazel near the Red Chief turnpike, — adjacent to the spot where an unknown body was lately discovered. This body is now strongly suspected to be that of one Henry Cass, a disreputable character, who has since been ascertained to have been one of the road agents who escaped. The matter is now under legal investigation. The successful result of the search is due to a systematic plan evolved from the genius of Mr. Beard, who has devoted over a year to this labor. It was first suggested to him by the finding of a ring, now definitely identified as part of the treasure which was supposed to have been dropped from Wells, Fargo & Co.'s boxes by the robbers in their midnight flight through Blazing Star.

In the same journal appeared the no less important intelligence, which explains, while it completes this veracious chronicle: —

"It is rumored that a marriage is shortly to take place between the hero of the late treasure discovery and a young lady of Red Chief, whose devoted aid and assistance to this important work is well known to this community."